STEPHANIE WATERS

W9-BRF-851

GHOSTS, LEGENDS, AND LORE OF THE ROCKIES

Schiffer Publishing Ltd

4880 Lower Valley Road · Atglen, PA 19310

Other Schiffer Books on Related Subjects:

Ghost Towns of the Rockies. Preethi Burkholder
ISBN: 978-0-7643-3569-3

Ghosts of Colorado. Dennis Baker
ISBN: 978-0-7643-3052-0

Copyright © 2018 by Stephanie Waters

Library of Congress Control Number: 2018934116

All rights reserved. No part of this work may be reproduced or used in any form or by any means—graphic, electronic, or mechanical, including photocopying or information storage and retrieval systems—without written permission from the publisher.

The scanning, uploading, and distribution of this book or any part thereof via the Internet or any other means without the permission of the publisher is illegal and punishable by law. Please purchase only authorized editions and do not participate in or encourage the electronic piracy of copyrighted materials.

"Schiffer," "Schiffer Publishing, Ltd.," and the pen and inkwell logo are registered trademarks of Schiffer Publishing, Ltd.

Designed by Brenda McCallum

Type set in Optima/Times Roman

ISBN: 978-0-7643-5569-1
Printed the United States of America

Published by Schiffer Publishing, Ltd.
4880 Lower Valley Road
Atglen, PA 19310
Phone: (610) 593-1777; Fax: (610) 593-2002
E-mail: Info@schifferbooks.com
Web: www.schifferbooks.com

For our complete selection of fine books on this and related subjects, please visit our website at www.schifferbooks.com. You may also write for a free catalog.

Schiffer Publishing's titles are available at special discounts for bulk purchases for sales promotions or premiums. Special editions, including personalized covers, corporate imprints, and excerpts, can be created in large quantities for special needs. For more information, contact the publisher.

We are always looking for people to write books on new and related subjects. If you have an idea for a book, please contact us at proposals@schifferbooks.com.

Dedicated to three grand dames,
whom I deeply admire for true grit:
Sherri Dupree, Judi Hinck (Marmel),
and to the Phantom of the Opera:
Thanks for the inspiration!

ACKNOWLEDGMENTS

Special thanks to Schiffer Publishing, especially to acquisitions editor Dinah Roseberry and rest of the editorial, production, and marketing teams. A heaping thanks to Madame X at the Tabor Opera House. Hats off to the Misfits, the Paranormal Peeps, and the Adventure Club. I couldn't have written this book without the help of Bix Moding and Wesley Waters, who helped with my haunted computer. Thanks to the following photographers: Dennis Alan Batchelor, Shaun Crusha, Jim Fliss, Cheryl Oney, Steve Sarutto, and Connie Sprague. Thanks for the interviews to Christopher Allen Brewer, Dori Spence, Jeanne Gripp, and Mrs. Tammy Taber. Thanks to my brothers Darin and Devin Waters for information on lakes and mining. Thanks to the Cimarron Hotel, Roger Pretti and Mrs. Tammy Tabor, and also Denver's Lodo Bar and Grill. My journey into self-fulfillment began after cancer, and I'm grateful to God for granting my bucket dreams!

CONTENTS

Preface 6

1. Phantom of the Opera 8
2. Ghost Rider of Cimarron 14
3. Fine, Young Cannibals of Heart Mountain 18
4. Revenge of Thunder Mountain 22
5. Skin Walker of Devil's Head 25
6. Séance at Fish Creek 29
7. Corpse Candles of Silver Cliff 33
8. Ghost Army of Spooky Sky Country 36
9. Hell's Bells of Cheyenne 41
10. Salty Ghost of Salt Lake 45
11. Witch of the Diablo Mountains 49
12. Truth of Old Man Mountain 52
13. Ghostly Lovers of Virginia City 56
14. Phantom Joyrider of Pueblo 60
15. Banshee Bride of Boot Hill 64
16. Fountain of Secrets 68
17. Shades of South Pass City 73
18. Haunted Heyburn Park 77
19. Time-Tumbling over the Overland Trail 80
20. Gloom of Dead Man's Gulch 84
21. Grim Reaper of Loon Creek 88
22. Ghouls Gulch 92
23. Curse of the Uintah Mountains 96

24. Resurrection at Isleta 99

25. The Queen's Haunted Mirrors 102

26. Ghost Riders of Loco Gulch 107

27. Monsters of the Lakes 111

28. Death Ship of the Platte River 114

29. Fountain of Love 117

30. Queen of the Damned 120

31. Sizzling Garnet 123

32. Spirits of the Merry Widow 126

33. Rogue of Rawlins 130

34. Bigfoot of Bishop Mountain 133

35. Crown Jewels of the Rockies 136

36. Yellowstone Fever 139

37. Ghost Waltz of Fort Union 142

38. Weird Curse of Manitou Springs 145

39. Fear of Sheep Mountain 149

40. Truth or Consequences and the Spanish Fly 152

Conclusion 157

Bibliography 160

PREFACE

Howdy Friends!

If you enjoy haunted history, then this, my fifth book, was written for you. I borrowed ideas for this project from the genius of journalist Charles Fort. Long ago, Fort became noted for his investigations into bizarre paranormal events. One such story was about falling fish from clear, blue skies. Fort interviewed eyewitnesses, finding that many of these accounts had logical explanations. However, the unsolved mysteries that he sensationalized made Charles Fort a household name. Like Fort, I focus on mysteries that took place long before imagination became homogenized, before Tinker Bell got the boot—at a time when opening minds were taken with the ideas of Ralph Waldo Emerson and Walt Whitman, both early leaders of this inspirational philosophy called transcendentalism. During western expansion, celebrated writers such as Ambrose Bierce manifested their destinies by stepping outside the proverbial box of traditional thinking. Taking a giant step for mankind, Bierce wrote a short story called "The Difficulty Crossing the Field," which demonstrated the early idea of traveling through time. Ironically, Bierce spent his last years in the southern Rockies before he suddenly vanished, and his last letter home ended with this mysterious line: "and as for me, tomorrow I leave for an unknown destination." Did the author disappear into the ether like the farmer who vanished while crossing his cornfield? We know Bierce studied transcendentalism and was greatly influenced by Native American mysticism, especially regarding their beliefs about Star-People. It's interesting to note that spiritual teachings about spacemen visitors took root thousands of years before Einstein theorized about relatively and the possibility of time travel.

I've always enjoyed consternating life and death's greatest mysteries. After being diagnosed with thyroid cancer, that passion became my life's work. So, I suppose it may have been my destiny to dust off the old newspaper archives and bring to light ancient mysterious long forgotten. Writing this book was especially thrilling when I became part of a ghost story! This mystery began in August 2016, when out of the blue I received a curious phone message from the Colorado Alarm Company about an intrusion signal at the Tabor Opera House Museum. I live nearly three hours away from Leadville, Colorado, and was really curious to know why they'd call me as the museum's emergency contact. So, within an hour I'd returned their call. But the alarm company had no recollection of phoning, and my private home number wasn't on their speed dial, nor was it remotely close to the emergency contact number. The mystery thickened when the next morning, I learned that the Tabor Opera House had just been sold to the city—saved from the wrecking ball! This was exciting news for history geeks!

But nobody at the opera house or at city hall had an explanation for my mysterious phone call from the Colorado Alarm Company.

So, I began thinking that perhaps the "Phantom of the Opera" was to blame. I've long believed the theater was haunted, and for good reason. Back in the spring of 1985, I'd gone to the Tabor Opera House to interview its current owners and had a bone-chilling paranormal experience. But I'd never shared my ghost story, because I didn't want folks thinking I'd gone bananas. Days passed and I couldn't stop thinking about my freakish experience there or of the mysterious phone call. Finally, I called a business associate, who is also a professional psychic-medium. Dori Spence didn't employ a crystal ball when she went into a trance, but her Tarot card reading told that I was destined to write about the opera house! Dori said I'd been beckoned because it was time to set records straight, so that the Phantom of the Tabor Opera House could finally rest in peace. She recalled how the Tabors were often betrayed in a negative light. But in actuality, they'd triumphed over great sorrow and were never given much credit. Mrs. Elizabeth Tabor was especially painted in unflattering colors, as a gold-digging home wrecker. Although nobody remembers to consider that she was an amazing artist and poet who left volumes of personal journals as testament to her strong spiritual faith and conviction, which came to be only after many years of atonement. Dori suggested it might have been my fate to draw a new picture of Mrs. Tabor. And I agreed with her astute observation, especially after realizing that both Mrs. Tabor and I were born lucky to be Irish, and on the seventh day of October, one hundred years apart!

All the stories in this anthology are about public places that you can actually visit. And these forty tales span from the lower Canadian Rockies to southern New Mexico. Herein lies the true cream of the crop: absolutely amazing stories about ghosts, UFOs, Bigfoot, time travel, doppelgangers, fate, omens, prophesy, witches, saints, sinners, vampires, miracles, and spontaneous human combustion. This project was three years in the making, as I tried visiting every place I wrote about. I had many fun adventures doing research and conducting interviews. Meeting local yokels and fellow haunted-history geeks was my favorite part of the ride. Hopefully, these supposedly true tales will take you on a journey of your own—one that might make you laugh or cry. Most of all, I hope you'll take the time to consider life's lessons within every tale and that you'll enjoy reading these timeless treasures as much as I did retelling them for your pleasure.

Happy Trails,
Stephanie "Windy" Waters

PHANTOM OF THE OPERA

When we remember we are all mad, the mysteries
disappear and life stands explained.

—Mark Twain

If you're looking for a stairway to heaven, it can be found in Leadville. Once the highest and most wicked mining camp known in the Rockies, it was home to only mountain goats and sinners . . . until the saints came marching in . . . and church bells rang from street corner to mountaintop. All were welcome in God's holy houses, save for the Witch of Fryer Hill. This strange creature had haunted those parts for longer than anyone could remember. Whispers told how she'd gone bananas from drinking well water poisoned by nearby metal mining. After nightfall she'd fly through back alleys snatching castaway treasures, always wearing a dark velvet cape, no matter what season. A floppy, black hat shadowed her face but still betrayed piercing peepers. If ever anyone caught a glimpse of the beguiling bag lady, they'd be mysteriously drawn to her like bees to honey. Some offered big bucks just to take her photograph or for an exclusive interview. But prying eyes and pesky requests were always promptly dismissed with the haughty wave of a ragged opera glove, or by a dry chicken bone.

Spring of '85 came much earlier than expected, bringing Mother Nature's resplendent bouquet of purple columbines, wispy bluebells, and, on the seventh of March, an urgent knocking upon the witch's door. And this sudden distraction caught her breath tight. Putting pencil and paper aside, she wondered if the sheriff was boarding her windows once again. But much to her surprise, it was a nosy reporter, who stumbled through swinging doors. "DON'T SHOOT," the young woman nervously stammered before gasping, "My name is Windy Waters—that's my nom de plume. I was sent by the newspaper. You see, I've always heard Leadville was haunted, and I'd love nothing more than to write a ghost story about this historic town. I suppose I'm looking for inspiration, seeking my ever-

Rare photo of the Phantom of the Opera.
Author's Collection.

elusive muse. But, having never been to this neck of the woods, I know not a living soul to interview. I've brought communion. Would you like to share words over French bread and wine?"

But her immediate response was only the patient click of an imposing grandfather clock. Until a woman appeared from parting shadows and softly demurred, "Bonjour Mademoiselle, now you're speaking my language! I'm Madame of the house, and I've long been expecting you."

A puzzled expression flashed over the newcomer's face. But before Windy could ask any questions, the little lady snatched away her jacket and hung it on a nearby hall tree.

After glancing around the dark corridor, Windy took quick mental notes of the eerie surroundings—and especially of her mysterious hostess. A childlike, pretty woman, with smeared rouge and lipstick, she looked like a china doll that'd been left in the rain. Wrapped high around her tiny head was a shiny, silver turban clasped by claws of a rhinestone peacock. Still another sparkling winged thing clasped at the full bosom of her white satin ball gown, which shimmered with silver sequins above black goulashes.

After winking into a wall mirror, the enigma signaled for her bewildered guest to follow her up a steep, grand staircase. As they climbed, golden glow from a handheld oil lamp spilled silently over each marble stairstep. Upon reaching the top landing, they entered a grand auditorium that was so quiet that you could have heard a pin drop. Regimented rows of cushioned, red-velvet seats sat stoically anchored by intricate black wrought ironwork. A solemn stage was cluttered with wooden wardrobe racks of costumes and crates spilling over with intriguing props. Dust blanketed the entire scene, as cobwebs dangled from the towering ceiling like Spanish moss.

As if on cue, a sharp beam of sunlight barged between velvet-draped balcony windows and fell center stage like a readied spotlight. With that heavenly invitation, the eccentric tour guide jumped into the silvery beam adding a broad smile. And after a girlish giggle and polite curtsey, she took a deep breath and bellowed,

Welcome to the Tabor Opera House. To be or not to be. That is the question. I'm still here because of pride, which tethers me here like a ball and chain. Long ago, this was God's country, until greed and mining forever changed the landscape . . . See that grand oil painting to the left of the proscenium wall? Well, that's Mayor Tabor, who made millions digging riches from the Matchless Mine and then built this elegant opera house. Horace spent a mountain of silver on this Ole Grand Dame. But Denver's high society dare not venture here because of its undesirous reputation, and so Mayor Tabor wisely rechristened Cloud City as the more prosperous sounding Leadville. Yes, Tabor's grand opera house soon brought inspiration along with an embarrassment of riches! Why, if these old walls could talk, they'd surely lament best of the bard's tragedies! Or whisper trade secrets of the Great Houdini! Humorist Mark Twain once pranced upon these boards and brought the house down with homespun wit . . . And speaking of absolute madness, building an elegant theater near timberline was considered a great financial risk. Yet, the Tabor Opera House became a huge success despite naysayers. Anybody who was anybody journeyed from afar to lofty Leadville. Most came in hope of meeting the forward-thinking Horace Tabor. But like all great men, he was tragically flawed . . . born with nothing and always wanting more. One day his wandering eye caught the attention of Elizabeth McCourt, a poor, little country bumpkin with a pretty face that could launch a thousand ships. Rumors were that she'd bewitched him, because it wasn't long before his slick attorneys procured a quickie divorce, without Mrs. Tabor's permission. And just as soon as ink was dry on divorce papers, Elizabeth and Horace had an opulent wedding like high society had never seen. Indeed, the lovebirds had everything money could buy, except for respect. With heads held high in the clouds, they left God's country and soon forgot where they'd come from. In Denver they found new friends with longer names and fancy titles. Once Horace became Lieutenant Governor of Colorado, red cotton long johns were no longer good enough. So, he began sleeping in $8,000 monogrammed silk PJs with diamond buttons! Not to be outdone, outlandish Mrs. Tabor paid $15,000 for their daughter's christening dress! And since Tabor's mining men worked in deplorable conditions and earned just three dollars for a hard, twelve-hour day, the pampered Tabors appeared insanely cold hearted . . . Like hungry ghosts, they'd become, always starving and aching for more . . . Take notice of that picture hanging on the wall to your right. That's Horace and Elizabeth scowling on their sprawling lawn. They built the largest castle on Denver's Capitol Hill, surrounded by a moat and a flock of squawking peacocks! And then they had the audacity to embarrass the blue-blooded neighborhood with gaudy, bronze statues of naked ladies! The three Graces stood back to back, shivering through rain, sleet, and hail. For ten glorious years, Horace and Elizabeth lived the high life, without a care in the world. Until the market suddenly crashed, gold became standard, and silver went out of style. Faith, Hope, and Charity were scattered by changing winds. Meanwhile, the Tabors found themselves with nothing but forgetful friends. Family turned their backs and refused to lend a helping hand. Everything they owned was auctioned to mow a mountain of debt. Horace eventually secured a humble job as a mailman, while they shacked up in a hotel. At least the lovebirds had each other . . . until Mr. Tabor suddenly died from an aching stomach, leaving his weary widow destitute and all alone in the world. Yet, just when she thought she could no longer bear another day of living hell, Elizabeth found strength in remembering her husband's ominous dying words . . .

"Hold on to the Matchless Mine! Having Faith, Hope, and Charity will make you a rich woman, once again!"

Although technically the Tabors no longer owned the abandoned Matchless Mine, Elizabeth took charity by squatting in the caretaker's cabin. For nearly fifty years, she drank bitter waters and shivered through long, cold winters, always hoping to find investors who believed the defunct silver mine could produce gold. Until one early spring, when faith smiled, and Elizabeth finally redeemed herself, becoming much richer than ever before! I've visited her grave a time or two. She's buried next to her beloved in Denver's Mount Olivet Cemetery.

Suddenly, the gong of Westminster's chimes long fully called from the lobby grandfather clock, and Windy sputtered, "Wow, time sure flies when you're having fun! But the bottle is empty and I'm sure your tongue is tired. I promise to return tomorrow. Thanks for the enchantment."

After grabbing her jacket from the hall tree, Windy hastened toward swinging doors just as the haggard voice trailing behind her quipped, "You're quite welcome, Mademoiselle. And by the way, I'm also a writer—my nom de plume is 'Baby Doe.' It's an endearing nickname from long ago . . ."

As promised, Windy returned to the Tabor Opera House, although it was much later than she'd originally planned. And so she wasn't much surprised when nobody answered her knocking. After pushing swinging doors open, she stumbled into the cold lobby and called down a dark corridor, "Hello, is anybody home?" But she was answered only by her own echo, and the faithful tick of a grandfather clock. So, she sat down to wait at a nearby ticket booth. Upon a table before her were stacks of notebooks. One journal caught her attention because it was labeled as *My Book of Visions and Dreams*. Inside held a treasury of artistic drawings, graceful poetry, and elegant musings of a literary genius—not the book of scribbled magic potions, evil spells, or mad ramblings that she'd somehow expected. But what really caught her eye was a yellowed newspaper article that fell into her lap. Ironically, the clipping was dated exactly fifty years earlier, with bold headlines that blasted:

BABY DOE TABOR
DIES AT HER POST
GUARDING MATCHLESS MINE

One-Time Queen of Colorado's Silver Empire

Faithful to the Last to Tabor's Injunction

Clad in Rags of Former Finery

Woman Sought for Beauty, Power, and Wealth

Lies Alone Two Weeks on a Bleak Frozen Hilltop

A Frozen Corpse . . .

According to the *Rocky Mountain News*, it was a good samaritan who'd discovered Baby Doe. This witness had gone to check on the hermit and told how the old mining cabin atop Fryer Hill had an eerie feeling as soon as she'd pushed her way inside. Mysteriously, she was greeted by the sweet fragrance of blooming flowers. A potbellied stove sat silent with cold ashes, and the one-room shanty was hushed by shadow. Stranger still was the vision of inexplicable, ethereal beauty: Baby Doe—sprawled upon the dirt floor with spindly arms outstretched like angel wings as if frozen in flight! And the old ragamuffin looked half her age! Much younger than eighty-one years. Clad in a withered, white ball gown and mining boots, with one tattered opera glove she'd clutched a silver crucifix. A tall turban crowned her tiny head like a silvery halo, while her sparkling, baby-blue eyes were turned upward in awaiting gaze. And while Mother Nature's alpine bouquet brought an early spring to Leadville, Baby Doe's cherubic smile had never melted. Windy couldn't stop staring at the eerie photograph. Until a resounding crash called from the lobby, and the distraction caught her by surprise. Pensively she walked toward the theater's entranceway, where she found the front doors had been flung wide open, and the sweet fragrance of flowers lingered. Her head began spinning so fast that she couldn't think. Frantically, she glanced up and down Harrison Avenue, calling for help. When to her great relief the glad call of church bells caught her ear, just as her eyes were drawn heavenward to an enchanting vision: a column of silvery clouds swiftly spiraling upwards . . . a miraculous stairway to heaven! While off in the distance, the gentle stir of spring winds carried a haggard voice cackling with laughter, as purple columbines and wispy bluebells easily swayed with glee.

Yes, Baby Doe finally found her stairway to heaven, which she'd climbed through inspiration of her own written words of atonement. And what about Windy Waters? Well, she had a story to write!

GHOST RIDER OF CIMARRON

... and behold a pale horse and his name that sat upon him
was Death, and Hell followed with him.

—Saint John of Patmos

Before New Mexico became the land of enchantment, it was better known as the land of illusions, and for good reason. Because whenever devilish winds blew, madness always followed. You could ask Henri Lambert about his frightful experience, but he's long been dead. Born in France, he was the White House chef for Abe Lincoln before relocating to Cimarron. Although he'd been warned about moving to the land of illusions, the Frenchman took a gamble and spent his life's savings on building a fancy hotel. Swanky bedroom suites dazzled the upstairs level, and downstairs was an eatery with thick tablecloths and thin soup. But locals were leery of swallowing anything they couldn't pronounce, and the Lambert Inn languished. Until a popular saloon was added. Satan's watering hole brought about a wicked crowd, and a terrible change in the formerly refined Frenchman, who began drinking and cussing like it was going out of style. And sophisticated Henri was never a dancer, until he began waltzing with the notorious outlaw Jesse James! Clay Alison was also a frequent dancer. In fact, he once jumped atop the bar and performed a drunken striptease for fellow outlaws Black Jack Ketchum and Wild Bill Hickok. As if overnight, Lambert's Inn became a wicked palace of sin and vice. Locals joked that murder at the Lambert was as common as the daily special, and how breakfast was always served with the grim report of who'd been gunned down the night before. Of course it wasn't long before the inn was avoided by everyone but those on the outs.

Then one fateful day, devil winds stirred yet another spray of drunken bullets. Sadly, an Apache boy running for cover was killed in crossfire. Prostrated with grief, Mrs. Lambert, a God-fearing woman, went to stay with consoling friends in Santa Fe. But before kissing her sinful husband goodbye, she warned of leaving him forever, if he couldn't save himself!

The Ghost Rider of Cimarron came to be identified as
T. J. Wright, and this is a rare photograph of the swindler.
Author's Collection.

A week later, devil winds swept a pale horse with a lone rider into town, and he looked meaner than a rattlesnake on a hot skillet! A gruesome, purple scar stretched from his nose to where an ear once hung, and his menacing, black grin was rotten from tobacco. At a barroom table, the stranger sat with his back to the wall, as his steely eyes fixed upon the swinging saloon doors. Well coifed, the lapel of his vest boasted a sparkling diamond stickpin as big as a Mexican jumping bean, and his fancy boots gleaned with a spit-polish shine. Until he was served, one black-leather glove drummed impatiently upon the tabletop while the other rested on the pearl handle of a splendid pistol. After casually sipping a glass of fine bourbon, the enigma paid for a single night's lodging and entrance to the special gaming tournament. But when Henri asked for the gambler's name, the newcomer shot a look that would sizzle Satan, and in gruff baritone, he sneered,

"Why, you can call me the Grim Reaper, Frenchie Boy! Because I'm here to take everything you love . . . including your mortal soul!" As the stranger strutted back down the hallway snickering to himself, Henri bemoaned, "Behold a pale horse and his name that sat upon him was Death, and Hell followed with him . . . the devil himself has blown into Cimarron!"

A few hours later, gamblers swaggered into the Lamberts' exclusive faro room. Cigars were lit and whiskey poured. Henri nervously held a handful of young clubs and lost the first round. And the next. All the while the man in black calmly chewed tobacco and joked about beginner's luck. But nobody was laughing. An hour into the game and Henri had already lost all his pin money. And then he lost his shirt, along with his fancy britches and new cowboy hat. Sweating in red long johns the shade of his face, he tried to look cool under pressure and was ready to slide under the table. Until finally, he was miraculously clasping a handful of faces. With a happy heart, Henri wrestled the golden wedding band off his pudgy finger and quipped "Here's to the Mrs.," and then tossed his ring onto the heaving table. Everyone roared with laughter except for the man in black, who'd slammed down yet another stack of crisp bills. But Henri suspected a bluff, and so he raised his bet once again by offering the only penny left to his name: the quick deed to his beloved Lambert Inn! Astonished players gasped in shocked disbelief and hastily folded. Except for the lone stranger, who countered by offering the quick deed to his rambling ranch! Tension was thicker than the cigar smoke. After an eternity of silence, the innkeeper slammed down his cards, roaring, "READ 'EM AND WEEP, BOYS!" But the man in black trumped with a winning hand calmly saying, "Look who's crying now!"

It was so quiet that you could have heard hell freezing over. Casually, the champion stuffed an immense fortune into readied saddlebags while snickering to himself. But before he'd reached the staircase, Henri staggered from behind the table and yelped, "Leave my hotel at once, stranger . . . or you'll be digging up daises before sunrise!" But, the man in black hissed, "Everything once yours is now mine!"

Well, my friends, those were fighting words. Within seconds a hail of gunfire came from behind and the bully froze, like a deer caught in headlights. Bullets ricocheted off the walls, as the winner stumbled to his knees and began crawling to his chamber. Moments later, Lambert and his henchmen pounded on the door to room #18, demanding a full refund! But the stranger cursed, "I'm never leaving . . . and if I die in this godforsaken hellhole, I promise to haunt this place, forevermore!"

The following morning, Henri remembered something about losing his hotel to a handful of face cards! After a swig of liquid courage, the brave innkeeper made his way upstairs, where he knocked on the door to room 18. After nobody answered, a readied passkey introduced him to a terrible sight. Upon the bed lay the mysterious stranger, in a puddle of dried blood. Wearing a frozen grin, his prying eyes seemingly followed Henri's every move. In quiet desperation, the terrified innkeeper got down on his knees to pray. And with tears flowing he swore to God that he'd never drink again! Now what happens to a man who makes a sacred oath and then breaks it? Well, my friends, Henri was about to find out . . .

A few weeks later, on the night of Mrs. Lambert's happy homecoming party, haunting footfalls were again heard coming from room 18! Henri rushed upstairs and pensively opened the door. The chamber was dark and quiet, and it stank of death. With a pounding heart, he pushed back his Stetson and squinted into the dim gaslight. Suddenly he recognized the scar-faced gambler lying on the bed! And before you could say Hail Lucifer, the Frenchman turned tail, slamming the door behind him!

In Satan's hellhole, Henri swallowed a sacred oath. And so he wasn't much surprised when the hauntings intensified. Night after night, terrifying footsteps could be heard stomping up the stairs and into the haunted room. These unwelcome visits frightened staff, and most walked off the job. Once word of the haunted inn got around the grapevine, business dried up and blew away like a tumbleweed. Making matters worse, the Grim Reaper soon took everything Henri had once loved—including his best hunting dog, his strongest pack horse, and even his devoted wife! The widower longed for sweet, merciful death . . . until one stormy night when he was awakened by his wife's familiar lilac perfume and heard her sweet voice whisper an idea on how to save his haunted hotel from certain ruin.

And so Henri soon put her plan into action. The next night, he hid in a broom closet while waiting for the ghost's faithful return. And after hearing the predictable stomping into room 18, the Frenchmen padlocked the door from the outside, thus trapping the menacing spirit inside! And with his troubles safely locked away, Henri found redemption by giving up the bottle and reembracing his Catholic faith. To celebrate life anew, the Lambert Inn received a fresh coat of heavenly white paint. Four hundred bullet holes were patched in the tin print ceilings, and new rules were posted against spitting, cussing, and killing. In line with his spiritual reformation, Henri renamed the Lambert Inn as the "Saint James Hotel." And all the positive changes soon brought about a more reverent and genteel crowd.

After nearly 150 years, the historic Saint James Hotel is still in operation. Not much has changed since the inn's reformation. New owners still honor old rules against spitting, cussing, and killing, and the long held tradition of keeping the phantom's room padlocked shut. Even so, spooky illusions stirred by devil winds still haunt the land of enchantment. But at least Henri's ghost isn't one of them.

FINE, YOUNG CANNIBALS
OF HEART MOUNTAIN

The way to a man's heart is through his stomach.
—Unknown

"Home is where the heart lives," as the old saying goes. And sometimes it's where the heart dies, especially on Heart Mountain. Home to a mysterious clan of native Indians, Heart Mountain was so named during a sacred ceremony, long ago. And according to archeological evidence it happened something like this . . . On a bleak night of the Hunter's Moon, naked warriors danced feverishly around a roaring bonfire as an anxious audience grew. And above this bedlam, a great king awaited in a lofty cave. Pounding drums echoed up the mountain slopes, keeping constant measure with his beating heart. Great was his vast kingdom, which began in the Owyhee Mountains and stretched down the lofty spine of the Rockies. His ancestors were known as the Ant People, and they'd helped the Hopi Indians find shelter before the great flood. His people were kind in those times. But one terrible day a ball of fire, the size of the sun, fell from the heavens and shook the earth. Scorched land poisoned the waters. Vegetation withered and died. Deer, bears, and buffalo ran far away, and his people soon followed. That is how his ancestors had arrived at Heart Mountain. Chief Tutu then stretched muscular legs before the dying fire. A shaman chanted prayers while shaking a medicine rattle to chase away evil spirits. Crushed berries, roots, and animal fat were compounded to create war paint in striking colors of ocher, crimson, and azure. A thin reed was used to brush sacred symbols onto dark, leathery skin. These mystical totems were known only to the wise ones, and their ancient wisdom had been passed from one generation to the next for thousands of years.

The fire crackled as beating drums reached a mighty crescendo, signaling that time for the sacred rite had come. Tutu arose from the cave floor with the grace of a panther. Illustrious silver streaks ran through his thick, black hair. His

Fine, young cannibals of Heart Mountain.
Author's collection.

deep eyes of ebony embers steamed with carnal passion. He was built strong, like a buffalo, and all the ladies thought Tutu was handsome. Perhaps that's why he had more wives than he could count. After entering the fading sunlight, the guest of honor stood upon a precipice that overlooked his vast empire. Heart Mountain was surrounded by thousands of warriors who'd traveled from the Four Corners just for the auspicious occasion. It was the great chief's birthday. A readied flag was waved, and billowing smoke signals rippled from camp to camp, signifying that the grand ceremony was about to begin.

Brave warriors lowered their eyes in reverence as the great Tutu stood before them. The chief waved to his loyal subjects and smiled as a royal buffalo robe was taken from his broad shoulders. Tutu sat upon a table of gold and proudly gazed over the crowd and into a setting sun. At his side were a dozen quivering maidens, awaiting the human sacrifice. An obedient sentinel waved his staff with great bravado until the mighty masses were silenced. And then, an unholy priest recited ancient prayers known only to the wicked. Circling from above, a black crow shrieked in horror, as a heavy rock mallet crashed down upon Tutu's awaiting skull. Crimson juice sprayed the audience, as the chieftain's head split open like a watermelon. Gleeful spectators roared with excitement, begging for an encore, and without missing a beat the holy man administered his talon-like fingernails and ripped open the chieftain's chest cavity. A beating heart was held high for all to see, and then the sadistic priest hastily devoured his happy prize! Excitedly, the masses chanted, "HEART . . . HEART . . . HEART," in cadence with pounding drums until a scarlet flag was waved overhead, for silence. From a precipice the holy man gazed over the "great unwashed," licked his crimsoned lips, and bellowed:

Forever remember this day on Heart Mountain! Dedicated to our great Chief Tutu, who was sacrificed for the betterment of our people, according to our ancient laws and customs. Only the strong can be warriors. Tutu was too old for life. In death he will be sealed in the sacred caverns of our ancestors. He has gone to the happy hunting grounds but will never be forgotten. On this special day, remember where you came from. Know that after the great fireball scattered our people to four strong winds, we were frightened babes in the woods. But since those dark days, we've grown strong. We've banded together, running great herds of buffalo off cliffs, and this abundance fed our families for many moons. But then meat grew scarce, and so we thrived by crafting poisoned arrows, killing the old, and feeding from the life of our enemies. Children are sweet, but we can't eat our own! And so, we became wicked warriors! We're fine, young cannibals who despise kindness and live only for ourselves. Youth and power have become our masters, and we will never again be at the mercy of our hated enemies: the Navajo, Cheyenne, Arapahoe, Sioux, Ute, Apache, Crow, Blackfoot . . . and we especially detest the Shoshone, who began calling us the Nimerigar, without our permission!

Upon mentioning their sworn enemies by name, the Nimerigar went wild! In a frenzy, the fine, young cannibals began biting one another with sharp, canine fangs and scratching at flesh with daggerlike claws. "HEART, HEART, HEART," they grunted, faster and faster, whirling like the dervish, pulling hair, and shaking tiny rattles. To be sure, it was pure bedlam. Little people can be scary, especially the cannibalistic Nimerigar, who in moccasins stand only six inches tall.

Fine, young cannibals, indeed they were. Shoshone Indians told that the Nimerigar were very wicked beings, and early-day pioneers also warned about these man-eating fairies. But by the late 1800s, most folks no longer believed in wicked Little People, naughty gnomes, or tricky trolls. Even gentle Tinker Bell got the boot. The world had changed; imagination homogenized.

And then came a big surprise, in 1932, when Cecil Main and Frank Carr were prospecting for gold and inadvertently discovered something much more valuable.

Inside a mysterious cave, they uncovered a little man of stone, the size of a banana, sitting cross legged in the lotus position upon a rock throne. Partially hidden under heavy lids were two huge, ebony eyes. And although the muscular, mummified man was older than dirt, it was easy to see that the peewee king had once been hunky and handsome. Plus he'd died happy—his thinly parted lips were frozen with a smile. An anthropologist examined various angles of x-rays and surmised that the tiny, rock man was a full-grown adult at only six inches tall. And he'd suffered a violent death, by a brutal blow to the skull. His collarbone was broken and his spine was cracked. Scientists named him Pedro, and after being dead for about 1,500 years, Tutu probably didn't mind the name change . . .

Pedro hit the road as center ring attraction at the circus and as a carnival headliner. Barkers hawked that Pedro was the progenitor of the modern human race, the missing link and eighth wonder of the world! Banners shouted PEDRO IS PREHISTORIC! PEDRO IS EDUCATIONAL! PEDRO IS COOL! VOTE FOR PEDRO! Curious audiences often asked, "Is Pedro related to fairies or gnomes? Could Pedro be from Mars? What's the deal with Pedro?" Out of the millions of questions, nobody ever asked why a miniature human being had fearsome canine teeth. But before these tantalizing questions could ever be answered, Pedro simply vanished into thin air. Was Pedro buried with Elvis back in August 1977 as the National Enquirer insisted? Who knows? Fame is fickle, my friends. This sort of thing happens all the time to flash-in-the-pan celebrities. One day you're hot, and the next you're not. In fact, the last time anyone saw Pedro, he was wearing a sandwich board, begging for loose change along the Hollywood Walk of the Formerly Famous.

However, some folks believe that Pedro returned to his former digs on Heart Mountain—perhaps for some good home cooking. After all, home is where the heart lives . . . And it's also where the heart dies, especially on Heart Mountain!

REVENGE OF
THUNDER MOUNTAIN

Ask not for whom the bell tolls, [perhaps] it tolls for thee.

—Ernest Hemingway

You can't fool Mother Nature, because she'll always get the last laugh. This lesson was learned long ago, on Thunder Mountain. This mountain was once home to the Sheep Eater Indians. Known for their mostly mutton diet, Sheep Eaters had long worshipped the mountain's many strange rock formations, including a colossal granite column known as the Sheep Eater's Monument. The natives believed that this sacred totem began as a puny pebble, but their love made the towering phallus grow taller with each passing year—until the 1870s, when the natives were chased away after white quartz veined with precious gold was discovered on Thunder Mountain. Thirst for this so-called "golden" salt lured prospectors to several mining hubs. The town of Roosevelt was a wild place, known for its eye-popping landmark that everyone called "Rosie." This colossal rock formation resembled a towering woman standing in the heart of town. Rosie's eyes were created by two dark holes, and wind-chiseled rivets appeared as flowing locks of auburn hair. Yet, discoloration in just the right spots made her look as naked as a newborn babe. Love-starved bachelors joked that their Amazon Queen was the perfect woman because she didn't talk much or wear clothes! And wherever there were funny guys, there had to be saloons. The first was roofed by blankets and a white bedsheet, which hung nearby with the word "Whiskey" scribbled in charcoal. Canvas tents and rustic shacks dotted the hillsides. Weary miners could sleep at the town's only boardinghouse, unless all the beds were taken, and then porch chairs could be rented for naps. The good ole boys were awfully happy when some hardworking gals arrived in town. They hung their shingle on Front Street, naming their business Dirty Sally's Hardware. Although the gals sold only screws, business was brisk, and life was rosy in Roosevelt.

The town of Roosevelt had a charming white chapel
with a bell tower that rang warning. *Author's Collection.*

One fine day, the mayor of Roosevelt shot at an eight-point buck. Happily
he hiked to retrieve his prize. But upon reaching the mountaintop he found a
half-naked man hovering over his dead doe. The bloody stranger held a buck
knife in one hand and a steaming liver in the other. Barefooted, and waist deep
in snow, he was wearing nothing but buckskin britches and a crimson smile.
After wiping blood from his long, gray beard, the freeloader mumbled apprecia-
tion for the hot lunch. A crazed look haunted his sunken eyes, and then in a
booming voice he blasted: "WE ARE MINION. LEAVE OUR SANCTUARY.
WINTER COMES AND DEATH FOLLOWS!" Swooping down from darkening
heavens came a squawking crow, and the lunatic ran after the messenger of death
until both disappeared from sight.

Indeed, the winter of 1901 was true to the prophet's ominous word. Sickness
and despair fell upon Thunder Mountain like a thief in the night. Yet, none of the
camps suffered more than Roosevelt. By November, the town was snowbound.
Grasses were buried deep. Game hunting was impossible. Animal feed ran dry,
and so stock animals were butchered. On Christmas morning, a starving man was
found murdered in the Roosevelt Saloon. He'd broken into a storage room and
was found splayed in a pool of warm blood, with a pickled egg protruding from
his mouth. Townsfolk callously agreed that he'd had it coming. Charity was
unthinkable, even on Jesus's birthday. And since they couldn't eat, they drank.
"Mountain Dew" was brewed from melted snow, plug tobacco, alcohol, and a
jigger of strychnine for a healthy heart. This powerful concoction put hair on a
man's chest and made him meaner than a sidewinder during molting season.
Barroom brawls were the only excitement they had to look forward to, and at

least a dozen men died from lead poising. All who perished remained where they fell, because the ground was too frozen for burials and survivors were too drunk to care. Cabin fever reached its zenith when townsfolk considered dining on the dead. Thankfully, spring finally sprung, and just in the nick of time. The first wagon headed out of town bore two living drivers and nineteen dead passengers. The ride cost a hefty fifty cents. Corpses without cash in pocket were unceremoniously tossed over a cliff.

Yet, despite inherent dangers, spring brought dream seekers who kept piling onto the lap of Thunder Mountain. Shady mining claims sold like hotcakes, and bitter lawsuits were filed with the Boise land office. This rash of indecency spurred the wrath of the crazy prophet, who returned for a second time. With great vehemence the holy man warned: "OH YE WICKED OF THUNDER MOUNTAIN . . . YOU SHALL SOON SUFFER LIKE THE BIBLICAL TOWNS OF SODOM AND GOMORRAH . . . ALL WILL PERISH, AND ROOSEVELT WILL SINK INTO HELL!" And then in the bat of an eye, the stranger went back to wherever he came from.

A town meeting was called and everyone agreed that Roosevelt needed a face lift. So, naked Rosie the stone Amazon Queen was dressed with a coat of white paint. Main Street was redirected around the colossal stone phallus. And at the far end of Roosevelt, townsfolk erected a charming chapel and churchyard surrounded by a white picket fence. Yet, everyone still thirsted for golden salt, and the blasting and ripping continued as usual.

Until one night when Thunder Mountain rumbled much louder than ever before. Around midnight, the church bell clanged rapid warning, which signaled a panicked exodus from Thunder Mountain. Wagons were hitched and horses saddled as blinding lightning ripped through inky skies. Shrieks and panicked cries pounded eardrums. It was every man for himself, as an avalanche of mud tumbled down, covering slopes, and the triumphant roar was heard as far away as Boise. At the meeting of Mule and Monumental Creeks, this avalanche left a mountain of debris that dammed the water's flow. Within hours, the entire town of Roosevelt easily sank into oblivion. Mother Nature rejoiced in triumph, as the Sheep Eaters Monument grew a few inches taller and Rosie the Amazon Queen cracked a Mona Lisa smile.

Today, legend tells us that Roosevelt Lake will never give up her dead. But at least all who perished provided food for the fish. Anglers often pull plump trout from steamy windows of Dirty Sally's. And I hear you can still get an aged bottle of Mountain Dew at the Roosevelt Saloon. Rusted tin mugs sway on arthritic tables as whipping waves jolt a player piano into clanking ragtime, and from the sunken church tower, a rusted bell clangs warning with each passing wave. This mournful calling beckons the phantom prophet to arise from his watery tomb. With phosphorescent buckskins glowing in the pale moonlight, the ghostly vision wanders the shoreline and preaches of being *fisher of men*. If you happen to see him, ask not for whom the bell tolls, because it might be calling for you! Such is the revenge of Thunder Mountain!

SKIN WALKER OF DEVIL'S HEAD

The Communication of the dead is tongued with fire
beyond the language of the living.

—T. S. Eliot

Even today, the mysteries of Devil's Head Mountain still live up to its name. One
of the strangest tales came about in October 1963, when a couple of cowboys
were sitting at the lunch counter of the Sedalia Café, and one said to the other:

Never go into the woods of Devil's Head alone. You should always bring
a friend. One that can't run as fast as you.

With a knowing nod, the other cowboy muttered:

Peggy Jones spied a grizzly along the ridge of Devil's Head. She told
that this beast was not your average bear, because it glowed in the dark,
had eyes that burned like hot coals, and scraggly fur, like porcupine quills!
One night Peggy spotted this brazen beast sipping from the Platte River.
She froze in her tracks and prayed . . . when the air crackled and smelled
of sulfur. Suddenly, the beast began laughing with a human voice, and Jones
ran for her life. But the brazen beast dashed over the river and caught her
by the heels, and that's how she got her peg leg. As a matter of fact, Peggy's
given name was Glades Jones.
Then there's the story of J. W. Langley. The rancher who nearly died of
fright after coming upon a huge, ten-point buck, seen on the mount. Again,
the monster glowed in the moonlight like a ghostly creature. With a steadied aim, Langley almost fired. But the ghost buck commanded in a booming, human voice that he lower his weapon! Langley obliged as if entranced.
Then of all the crazy things, the big bully spat in his face and called him a

coward! So he rode into Sedalia like his underpants were on fire! Nobody believed his ridiculous story. Judged insane, Langley was sent to the Cracker Box Palace!

We also know that Devil's Head is home to lost treasure. Long ago, the Collins Gang buried a Well's Fargo box of Gold Eagle coins and it's never been recovered. But there's no way in hell you'd ever catch me hunting in those haunted woods!

Suddenly, an old campaigner hobbled up to the serving board, saying:

Pardon my pudding boys, but I'm an expert on that monstrous mountain. So put on your listening ears and maybe you'll learn something! Long ago, I pulled up my tent stakes along Cherry Creek and moved to Devil's Head country. You could say that Devil's Head had beckoned me like a sailor is called to the sea. With only a wagon of supplies, a cow, mule, and my worthless watchdog, Pancake, I made my way through the rugged wilds of Jarr Canyon. In a wooded forest known as Indian Flats, I cleared a solid plot to build upon. An ideal location, as nearby swampy lands furnished my beasts with natural fodder. I chopped wood and carried water. Mud for mortar I'd chinked between the log walls. My cozy cabin soon became home sweet home. I hate to toot my own horn, but you'll never meet a more skilled mountain man than myself. Why, I can track bees through a blizzard or a whisper in the winds. I trapped deer and elk. Most of the hides I'd cart into town and trade for flour, coffee, and tobacco. I collected wild honey, mushrooms, roots, and berries, which always brought fair pocket change. Sure, I'd pan for gold along the Platte. But after saving up enough money to purchase my new muzzle loader, hunting bear became my passion. One morning, I shouldered my rifle, whistled for my dog, Pancake, and then off we went hunting grizzly. Over the hills we tramped. My moccasin boots barely made a peep as I tiptoed over crunchy, yellow granite. After two miles we struck out upon a long ridge, dividing the watersheds and leading toward the needled points of Devil's Head.

Knowing bears as I do, I hoped to find one sleeping in the airy labyrinth of trees. Once I stepped under the quaking, golden canopy, a cool welcoming breeze stirred the sweet smell of balsam through the air. Bears make their homes where mountain ash and scrub maple mark the center of the draws. So, I found a boulder to sit upon and enjoyed my lunch of buttermilk biscuits and baked beans. Suddenly, Pancake growled like he meant business, and a familiar feeling crept over me. The hair on the back of my neck stood up as prickles ran down my spine. While kneeling in prone, I carefully loaded my piece, measured powder in the palm of my hand, and selected a round slug. Then I pointed the muzzle toward the

Devil's Head became known for talking animals called Skin Walkers.
Author's collection.

draw on my left. It was so quiet . . . From the corner of my eye, I spied a large, hairy beast shuffling through the bushes. Without looking twice, I turned and pulled a faithful trigger. Through the foliage I saw a mighty monster tumble. Its legs kicked before falling with an exhausted thud. But before retrieving my happy prize, something terrible happened. I heard a peculiar sound coming from the felled beast. It, the monster, I mean to say, was shrieking with a human voice! But then this unholy sound soon turned to maniacal laughter, which was both awful and fascinating. I was dizzied and broke into a cold sweat. Blood drained from my face and I was sick to my stomach. The bully had vanished!

Frightened as hell, I ran in the opposite direction. But just then, from behind a granite boulder, came this insidious monster! Not a bear, but a huge buck, the likes of which I'd never seen! Twice the size of a full-grown elk, with huge antlers like twisted branches of an old piñon tree! An ethereal silver coat glowed over its kinky fur, which was standing on ends! Its expression was terrible and nearly impossible to describe. All I know is that it was a wild animal, yet human. So I held my breath and said my prayers. The Goliath turned its frightful head, and horrible eyes flashed with fire and smoke as they gazed into mine. I felt as though he could read my thoughts!

With trembling hands, I reloaded my rifle. My heart pounded as cold sweat dripped from my brow. I feared the powder wouldn't explode, and I'd be left to the mercy of this vile creature. With trembling hand, I dropped another ball into the barrel. When I looked up, the buck's terrible eyes were still upon me. No doubt he was calculating my every move. His lips curled inward, exposing fierce canine fangs. Clouds of steam flared from his billowing nostrils, and it sent shivers down my hide. And then of all crazy things, the terrible creature grinned from ear to ear, mocking my fear. But I took a deep breath, caught him in my cross hairs, and fired.

The thundering shot punched sunlight into the buck's liver. But much to my surprise, not a drop of blood spilled from the gaping wound. Adding to my dismay, the hideous monster stood like a stone statue, never blinking an eye! After an eternity of silence, it winked at me, and then moseyed away with head held high. I was too frightened to follow. But as I ran toward my cabin, I heard its wicked laughter off in the distance, and my blood ran cold!

That night, as I lay awake in bed, I recalled an old Navajo legend that I'd learned at my grandfather's knee. It was about the Yee Naaldlooshi. In English they are known as "Skin Walkers" or "Shape Shifters." These creatures are ghosts of evil shamans, who travel through time and morph into various creatures by wearing skinned animal hides like a cloak. When in animal form, you can still see that they're human because they'll talk with a human voice. After pondering the evidence, I came to believe that the Ghost Buck of Devi's Head was indeed a fearsome Skin Walker!

During the West Creek mining boom, tales of shape-shifting creatures were popular around huddled campfires. Eventually, the *Rocky Mountain News* blew the whistle on the spooky creatures of Devil's Head, and since it was written in the newspaper, you know it has to be true! Well, I'd better head back to my tipi, before the sun sets and they roll up the boardwalks. But it's been a pleasure chewing the fat with you fine fellas!

The old man then swallowed his last drop of coffee and limped out the door, never to be seen again. Even so, he'd never be forgotten. Because a tip he'd left on the bar top turned out to be a rare and very valuable Gold Eagle coin! And on the floor? A trail of mud tracks—shaped like animal hooves! And now you know why Devil's Head Mountain will always live up to its frightful name.

SÉANCE AT FISH CREEK

Blood is thicker than water.

—Modern proverb

Blood is thicker than water, except at Fish Creek. This came to be known in October 1880, when hundreds of Basque sheepherders gathered in the Bitterroot Mountains, along the grassy banks of Fish Creek. The king of the gypsies had a beautiful daughter, and she was to be married to the prince of a rival family. This prearranged match would unite warring clans and bring peace for generations to come. In preparation for the grand celebration, sheep were slaughtered and fresh bread was baked over busy campfires. Life was squeezed from the squawking throats of mallard ducks in order to create hot blood pudding. Although this traditional Basque wedding dish was barley palatable, it promised to bring good luck to the beloved couple.

But this gypsy wedding broke all the rules. Once the drunken groom arrived, he saw red and slashed the jugular of his handsome brother. Before the trembling bride could scream in protest, she too was silenced by the stroke of a jealous blade. Alas, the groom's ugliness was terrible to behold. Riddled with guilt, he slit his own throat and then jumped into the churning waters of Fish Creek! And what was to become a joyous, new beginning was silenced in a heartbeat.

Wedding guests were horrified. Some ran for the hills while others began fighting to beat the band. When all was said and done, the dead far outnumbered the living. Yes, it was a terrible bloodbath. And, as the golden sun set over the Bitterroot Mountains, Fish Creek ran red with blood. (At least hungry fish enjoyed the bountiful harvest.) Not long after the tragedy, those troubled waters became better known for ghosts than for *cutthroat* trout. And over time, everyone shunned Fish Creek except for those who didn't know any better . . .

In 1915, a Canadian couple and their adopted daughter moved into an abandoned cabin on Fish Creek. But just as soon as the McDonalds rolled out the welcome mat, ghosts came calling. Ten-year-old Mary Ellen was the first to be haunted. One night she awoke screaming from her attic bedroom. Entranced, she mumbled of being touched while sleeping. After searching through the blankets, her parents were relieved to find that the offending trespasser was only a squeaky mouse. Causing much-greater concern was the spirit board stashed under her mattress.

"Where did you get this evil thing," demanded her red-faced father. But before the wide-eyed girl could answer, he took a deep breath and bellowed; "Mary Ellen, if I've told you once, I've told you a thousand times . . . you are not to horse around with spirit boards, Tarot cards, or crystal balls. Occult devices belong in the devil's workshop. Now, go throw that despicable thing on the fire, and then I don't want another peep out of you—or from that confounded mouse!"

Obviously, Mr. McDonald was daft about laws of the supernatural, because any fool knows you should never burn a spirit board, since it will always bring the devil's wrath! Low and behold, the very next morning mysterious shenanigans plagued the farm. Like when Mary Ellen went to milk the cows, they refused her gentle approach and kicked at their stalls.

Teary eyed, Mary Ellen returned to the kitchen with an empty pail. Her mother was hungry for breakfast and wasn't in the mood for childish games. Mrs. McDonald grabbed Mary Ellen by the shoulders and sneered, "I suppose you're going to blame Mighty Mouse. Come with me and we shall milk the cows together!"

As mother and daughter marched toward the barn, static electricity crackled through the air, and, yet, the entire scene was eerily still, like the calm before a storm. Upon opening the barn doors, they stood in silent wonder. Smoldering tension quickly turned to suspicion.

After shaking her head in disgust, Mrs. McDonald took a deep breath, put her hands on her hips, and scolded, "Did you release the cattle out of spite? Go to your room, young lady, before I send you back to the orphanage!"

A few hours later, Mary Ellen's parents had just returned the last cow to the barn, when they spotted smoke coming from their farm house. The couple raced to douse the flames before the blaze caused much damage.

"What happened?" demanded Mary Ellen's angry father.

The girl looked up to meet his eyes and sheepishly stuttered "I don't know papa. I was just sitting on my bed . . . I couldn't move . . . I felt like I was someone else, watching everything from a dream. I'm sorry. Please, don't be angry!" The little girl rushed into her father's loving arms and all was forgiven.

That evening the family was enjoying supper when a strange scratching sound shattered the peaceful moment.

"Must be that damn mouse again," grumbled Mr. McDonald and then playfully teased "Maybe he should start paying rent!"

Laughter broke the tension, but not for long. Around midnight, the couple was alarmed when once again, shrieks came tumbling from the attic. After rushing upstairs, Mary's mother found her daughter standing on the bed, naked as a newborn babe. The girl stuttered that she was awakened by wicked laughter. Bedcovers and then her nightgown were ripped away! She screamed and ran for her bedroom door! But she didn't get far because something that was unseen picked her up and slammed her to the floor! Mary's mother wrapped her weeping daughter in a blanket and comforted her the best she could. And then while rocking the trembling child in her arms, Mrs. McDonald suddenly shrieked! Because a log ceiling beam painted in dripping red letters simply said: *HELP!* And there was no way that Mary Ellen could have reached the lofty beam without a ladder.

Over the following months, things went from bad to worse. Livestock shuffled from one barn to another, although the doors remained latched from the outside. Heavy farm equipment moved across the fields on their own volition. Loud knocking and rapping on the walls continued night and day. One morning, while the McDonalds were eating breakfast, a burning match fell from the ceiling and landed on the girl's lap. Thankfully her quick-thinking mother doused the flames. A week later, Mr. McDonald smelled something burning and ran upstairs to find a pile of his daughter's clothes smoldering in the center of her room. At the same moment Mrs. McDonald spied smoke coming up from the floor. So, she rushed downstairs to find a mound of wood shavings blazing in the root cellar. The next day, a wet sponge caught fire while soaking in a bucket of mop water. Six cows died in the barn without apparent cause. Tension mounted and the family bickered constantly. Finally, Mary Ellen was sent to live with neighbors for a brief respite. During this time, everything was as cool as a cucumber. But just as soon as the witchy girl returned, paranormal activity followed. News of Mary Ellen's supernatural talent spread throughout the countryside, and she soon became known as the Ghost Girl of Fish Creek.

Locals feared venturing anywhere near the accursed Spook Farm. Mary Ellen's parents worried about their witchy daughter, and so they called on an expert. From the University of Montana came the distinguished professor Dr. Thaddeus L. Bolton. His three-man team agreed to live with the family on their remote farm for one entire week. Everyone, including the McDonalds, slept on the floor in front of the fireplace. Each night séances were held before a knowing fire. Amazingly, foreign voices, shaking tambourines, and mournful mandolins were heard. They also saw fleeting figures that glowed and danced in the dark.

But the biggest surprise came after the investigation team had their film developed. Several prints showed everyone while they were bundled on the floor sleeping. Needless to say, the scientists were baffled, since the cabin door had been bolted from the inside and the McDonalds' watchdogs never whimpered at an intruder. Stranger still was that some prints showed a misty woman wearing a flowing white wedding gown. Front-page headlines for the *Anaconda Standard* screamed about the ghost of a weeping bride being heard, seen, and photographed at Fish Creek, and the news spread from sea to shining sea. A month later, the cabin at Fish Creek burned to the ground, and Mary Ellen's family moved far, far away. But that wasn't the end of the spooky girl . . .

Seven years later, a teenager named Mary Ellen McDonald made international news when her farmhouse along a Canadian river in the northern Rockies became plagued by paranormal activity. During the summer of 1922, over thirty spontaneous fires erupted at so-called Spook Farm. The strange happenings captivated the public's imagination with international headlines warning about the "Antigonish Ghost." A team of world-famous scientists and paranormal investigators, including Sir Arthur Conan Doyle, soon arrived on the scene. Several astonished witnesses reported being slapped on the face and feeling an unseen force watching them. One scholar suggested that radio waves were causing the paranormal

This cabin on Fish Creek was haunted by a band of gypsy ghosts before it burned to the ground. *Author's Collection.*

phenomena. But famed Italian wireless inventor Guglielmo Marconi claimed radio waves weren't capable of igniting spontaneous fires. An anonymous donor offered a staggering $100 reward to anyone who could find a logical explanation. But the big-brained scientists never found a plausible excuse for the paranormal activity.

After Mary Ellen's second farmhouse burned to the ground, she was shipped away. Albeit not to the orphanage. She was sent off to the Cracker Box Palace. In the adjoining cell, Napoleon fought battles and Shakespeare wrote bestsellers. However, Mary Ellen's only talent was starting fires without matches . . . and talking to ghosts!

Meanwhile, the distinguished Dr. Thaddeus L. Bolton was promoted to head of the Psychology Department at Temple University in Salt Lake City. His report about the Ghost Girl of Fish Creek was published in the *Rocky Mountain News.* Paranormal investigators searched through newspaper archives and discovered that the gruesome story about the ill-fated gypsy wedding and then the terrible hauntings at Fish Creek made perfect sense. Even so, Mary Ellen never again saw the light of day, as she spent the rest of her life imprisoned at the Dartmouth Asylum for the criminally insane.

Blood is thicker than water, except at Fish Creek. Churning waters cleansed the bloody bloodbath long ago. Yet, restless spirits of the gypsy wedding still remain tethered to where they died. And like a ball and chain, love and hatred have become their everlasting despair.

7

CORPSE CANDLES OF SILVER CLIFF

Remember, friends as you walk by, as you are now,
so once was I. Just like me you will someday be, so prepare
yourself to follow into eternity.

—Tombstone epitaph

Yes, the Wet Mountains are terribly haunted. The most-famed ghosts in them hills are a restless pair of fighting phantoms. This frightful ghost story was published back in August 1878, when, as luck would have it, all the boardinghouses in the town of Silver Cliff were occupied. And so, hopeful miner Duke Drake made his way to the outskirts of town. Happily he discovered an abandoned shanty. After enjoying a simple meal of dried meat and corn dodgers, he rolled his bedsack over a dirt floor and was soon counting sheep. He dreamed of striking it rich, until haunting music shattered tranquility. This midnight serenade came from somewhere in the dark room. A storm began brewing as flashes of lightning briefly illuminated the chamber. When suddenly, two fearsome strangers emerged from dark shadows! Both were dressed like miners, but their bodies were transparent and glowed with an ethereal phosphorescence! Swinging punches, these phantom figures desperately fought in violent struggle. Perspiration dripped from furious faces as they moved gracefully, without a sound. The paranormal players continued their brutal battle while never acknowledging their spellbound witness. Rain poured from the heavens as thunder trumpeted from the horn of Gabriel. Quaking like a leaf, Duke pulled a blanket over his head and huddled in the corner, transfixed with fear. Suddenly, one phantom turned toward its horrified witness. A flash of lightning illuminated the room. After peeking out from under the blankets, Duke instantly recognized his childhood chum by the name of Hal Crawford! In quiet desperation he tried to bolt from his bedroll and help his troubled friend. But invisible chains held him tight. After an eternity of silence, Duke somehow summoned strength and sprang from the floor. But the apparitions vanished into thin air! Stranger still was the pearl-handled dagger left lying on the floor! Engraved on the blade were the initials H. C., and Duke's head began to spin because it was the exact same dagger that he'd given his buddy Hal Crawford three years prior!

With a pounding heart, Duke saddled his horse and rode back into Silver Cliff, hell-bent for leather. At the Buffalo Saloon he poured his heart out to a big-eared bartender who recognized the elegant, pearl-handled dagger. And he told that three years earlier, how a stranger stumbled into Silver Cliff and built himself a cabin near the end of town. But shortly thereafter, he was found murdered. Outside his cabin, a dying Spaniard told of their deadly altercation. They'd gone to blows over a jumped mining claim. Their corpses had so many stab wounds that they looked like pin cushions. Yet, the murder weapon had never been found. The hated rivals were buried at the new Silver Cliff Cemetery, where they share a common grave.

Shortly after their burial, flickering silver balls of light known as "corpse candles" began haunting the boneyard. Locals claim that these angry spirits are of Duke and the Spaniard, who still battle in the great hereafter. Folks believe that they haunt the old boneyard because the doomed enemies hate sharing a common grave.

Legend tells that if you walk through the cemetery at the stroke of midnight, mysterious harmonic music will send shivers down your spine. This haunting serenade comes from the ghost of Duke. His haunting melodies always begin at a slow pace, like the gentle murmur of a summer zephyr in a pine forest. Then the tempo increases until it resembles an eerie wailing. After the strange serenade begins, ghost lights flicker and they swirl above the ground and dance among the tombstones.

One night, over fifty witnesses reportedly saw the spine-tingling spirit dance. As eerie harmonica music whistled and townsfolk tried catching mysterious, dancing lights. But the fleeting phantoms played hide and seek by disappearing and then reappearing in other sections of the boneyard . . . like they had an intelligent consciousness.

As word spread about the haunted graveyard, the town of Silver Cliff experienced a renaissance. Professional psychics came from around the world just to investigate the haunted boneyard. In 1968, Silver Cliff got international press attention when *National Geographic* magazine came calling. Their article confirmed that the spooky reports were true, but they still couldn't logically explain the bizarre occurrences.

Even today, the dead of Silver Cliff far outnumber the living. Most residents of the living ghost town know their infamous boneyard is uniquely haunted. However, a few smarty-pants types support a more logical explanation. They argue that the graveyard soil has a high concentration of bentonite, an absorbent clay. Once bentonite becomes moist (as it often does in the wet mountains), it causes the earth to slip and slide. Furthermore, moist bentonite makes anything buried sprout from mud like the first crocus of spring. And the corpse candles? Well, naysayers claim that the ghost lights are nothing more than phosphorescent gases, arising from decaying corpses. Even so, nobody can explain the pathetic screeching that still resonates from Duke's phantom harmonica.

So, the town of Silver Cliff finally embraced their paranormal problem, rather than trying to fix it. City leaders initiated the annual Haywire Blue Grass Festival, where the phantom musician is the guest of honor. Once again, the dying ghost town was resurrected from the dead. Ghost hunters came from all over the country to see the infamous ghost lights of Silver Cliff along with the rusty, pearl-handled dagger, now on display in the town museum. Fighting phantoms isn't something you see every day, and the same can be said of this ghostly dagger. And now you know why the Wet Mountains are still considered to be very haunted, even after all these years.

GHOST ARMY OF SPOOKY SKY COUNTRY

Vision is the art of seeing things invisible.
—Jonathan Swift

Could the heavens be haunted? Paranormal investigators would answer yes! Especially the big skies over Montana, where mystical images have long been seen. This mysterious phenomenon began in June 1876, when Chief Sitting Bull stood proud upon a hilltop overlooking a sea of tipis and bellowed:

> We give thanks to the Great Spirit for making us human beings and for our victories and for our defeats . . . We are grateful for vision of what's seen and unseen . . . Twelve moons ago, a white buffalo was born along the Red River. We know this to be a sign from the Great Spirit. This birth foretold of troubled times for our people. Since then, many have been forced off our homelands and onto reservations. We have been made to cut our braids because overseers say that short hair was more sanitary . . . and more fashionable. They take away our buckskins and throw them onto a fire, and then we are given ugly, starched garments. Our tribal names are thrown to the winds and we are given Christian names, which mean nothing. We are expected to forget native customs and languages. They want us to look like them, be like them, and think like them. But why? How are we to support ourselves with farming when the soil is bad? Our crops failed, and we weren't given promised grain. Many starved and died. Why does the white man speak with forked tongue? Even our gods, they say are wrong. Uncle Sam fears our sun dance, so he made practicing this sacred rite a crime—punishable by death. But I am here to say that we will no longer allow this shameful tyranny. We will call

upon our ancient ancestors through our sacred sun dance and they will join in our fierce battle against the hated white man!

Chief Sitting Bull looked down from the stone precipice and triumphantly raised his mighty spear as thousands of Sioux, Arapahoe, and Cheyenne warriors roared with great enthusiasm. This grand army united bronzed brothers with a common beef against their dreaded enemy. Some of these fearless renegades had already escaped from Uncle Sam's new Indian reservation system. It was the largest powwow that anyone had ever seen. For three days, warriors shook powerful medicine rattles and pounded noble war drums. Magic and mystery filled the air. This loose confederacy had gathered along the Rosebud Creek in the Dakota Territory with the pretense of performing the sacred sun dance.

In preparation for the holy rites, the big chiefs fasted for several days. An offering of flesh was needed for their war god *Wakantaka*. So, Sitting Bull took a sharpened bone and gouged chunks of bloody flesh from his already weakened body. He scooped fifty pieces from each arm, and then two bone hooks were pierced through each of his nipples. While the crowd chanted, the great chieftain was hoisted above the sweat lodge, where he dangled from a towering pine pole. As his many wounds dripped onto dancing warriors below, the solemn rhythm of drums kept steady cadence. In his native tongue, Sitting Bull chanted, *"Hoka hey! Nake'nula waun welo unpe'tu kin le' mat'in kta hechhetuwala!"* meaning "live long and remember . . . the fight keeps on." As streams of crimson red trickled down his bronzed arms and muscular legs, the holy man stared into the dizzying heavens and witnessed a profound vision. Between hovering clouds he could see individual tipis pitched along a river. It was early morning and squaws were cooking over campfires while laughing children played within reach. Sioux braves were watering horses when mists suddenly parted with a thunderous clap and hundreds of white soldiers charged horses toward a peaceful village of natives. The army was led by a fearless warrior who had flowing locks of yellow hair. Curiously, Sitting Bull envisioned the invading cavalry as riding upside-down in their saddles. But it was a great battle. White soldiers fell from the heavens like grasshoppers. After about ten minutes, the illusion slowly faded into the clouds. Sitting Bull took this vision as an undeniable sign that war was imminent and that his people would prevail over tyranny.

After the sun dance, several chieftains met in the grand tipi. A special peace pipe filled with magical herbs was passed around the sacred circle, and the shaman told them it was big medicine. A swirl of sage smoke spiraled upward through the tipi's ventilation hole and peacefully drifted away from the encampment—over rivers and mountains, through forests and desserts, until it oozed into the windows of Fort Abraham Lincoln.

"What's that strange odor I smell?" asked one soldier to another, adding, "Whatever it is, it's burning my eyes and throat—the winds must have brought smoke from a distant prairie fire. What do you think, General?"

An army of ghostly warriors haunt the skies over Montana.
Author's collection.

George Armstrong Custer nodded in agreement before pulling a red silk scarf from around his neck, wiping teary blue eyes. After a few rapid blinks he shook his illustrious, golden locks and replied, "It stinks—shutter the windows!"

At the age of thirty-six, Custer was famous for his stellar military career. He'd been called the "Boy General," since he was still wet behind the ears. In fact, his astute military prowess is why he'd been selected to lead a courageous crusade against the renegade Indians.

The following morning, Custer and the 7th Cavalry marched away from Fort Abraham Lincoln with murderous hearts. However, the dawning sunlight caused an uncanny mirage to appear in the morning sky. Over fifty wide-eyed witnesses watched in horror as a reflection of the soldiers' regiment divided into three separate lines. Rather than being a stationary mirage, it was more like a motion picture. And this grand-scale production reenacted for a full eleven minutes before the soldiers were sucked behind a curtain of clouds, which closed the show. A huddled crowd was spellbound. Especially Mrs. Elizabeth Custer, who feared that the heavenly apparition was as an evil omen and that it would be the last time that she'd ever see her beloved husband. Adding to her anguish was that as the brigade marched away, the buglers played a haunting song that pulled at her heart strings—a popular little ditty known as *The Girl I Left Behind*:

If ever I get off the trail and the Indians, they don't find me
I'll make my way straight back again, to the girl I left behind me.
Oh, that girl, that purdy little girl, the girl I left behind me
With rosy cheeks and curly hair, the girl I left behind me . . .

Sitting Bull, Crazy Horse, and Chief Gall must have created some very powerful mojo during their spirited sun dance, because the Battle at Little Big Horn became their greatest triumph. Military strategists and historians are still perplexed as to what exactly happened that fateful day. But we do know that Custer was acting at least somewhat deranged, since he made some terribly senseless mistakes. Perhaps his biggest snafu was leaving the 7th Cavalry's Gatlin guns (rapid-firing weapons) behind at Fort Abraham Lincoln, saying that they were too cumbersome and would delay their journey. And then, just before arriving at the Little Big Horn River, the Boy General sent three Pawnee scouts to investigate the nearby Indian encampment. These agents reported that the 7th Cavalry was greatly outnumbered, and advised Custer to wait for reinforcements. They also warned against dividing the cavalry into three separate troops, since this plan of attack would further weaken their numbers. But Custer responded to this wise advice by bellowing, "We will take no prisoners, especially not the squaws, as they breed like rabbits!" But, the yellow-haired general gravely underestimated the Sioux, Arapaho, and Cheyenne warriors, who had a combined force of ancient supernatural powers working in their favor. Legend tells us that by performing their sacred sun dance, the native warriors had become invisible to the eye, and their army of native warriors became like a whisper in the wind! This explains why many of Custer's men soon threw down their weapons in uncontested defeat against unseen warriors. It was a bloody battle, and the few soldiers left standing begged to be taken captive. The unrelenting ghost army of Sioux, Arapahoe, and Cheyenne warriors, however, showed no mercy.

The Battle of the Greasy Grass, also known as Custer's Last Stand, was over in a heartbeat. Nearly 300 white soldiers were ruthlessly slaughtered by an army of unseen. Lakota legend tells that once the crazed general realized he'd been defeated, he used his own gun to kill himself; a single bullet hole was found in his left temple. However, nobody really knows for certain, since dead men don't talk. Curiously, Custer's body was the only corpse found on the greasy battlefield that wasn't mutilated. In fact, his corpse wasn't recognized at first, because the Boy General wasn't wearing a military uniform. Eventually, Custer was identified by his lovely locks. Given that the general was famed for his golden curls (which he proudly scented with expensive cinnamon oil), it was highly unusual that his honey-colored hair wasn't scalped as a prized trophy. But then again, Sioux, Arapahoe, and Cheyenne warriors weren't known for scalping enemies who they suspected as being crazy, because they feared releasing evil spirits trapped inside their head. The natives likely thought Custer was mentally deranged for impulsively attacking their encampment, knowing that his troops were greatly outnumbered. Meanwhile, back at Fort Abraham Lincoln, Mrs. Custer promptly fainted at 4:00 p.m., which was about the same time that her beloved general fell from his horse . . .

Although the Sioux, Arapahoe, and Cheyenne won the Battle of Big Horn, they soon lost the war. Chief Sitting Bull and Crazy Horse were assassinated by US soldiers, just weeks after their supernatural triumph at Little Big Horn. Soon thereafter, their people were marched off to Indian reservations. Those who didn't cooperate were executed.

But the natives had the last laugh, because the indelible magic from their spirited sun dance lingered long after the cry of war drums was silenced. Witnesses told that spooky apparitions could been seen on the battlefield and in the sky. On October 21, 1882, the *Helena Weekly Herald* quoted a resident as saying:

A great shadowy picture of an encampment of soldiers hung way off there in the sky. I could see a rapid river, with a good- sized creek coming into it from a rocky canon in the mountains behind. On the bank, which was grassy and level, were several large white tents . . . a number of smaller ones and others were being put up by soldiers . . . Horses were being unsaddled by men who seemed to have just come, as a crowd was gathered around them . . . Some animals were rolling around just beyond the line of tents, and a half dozen men had four or five horses each down to the river's edge where they were giving their horses a drink. Two campfires were being started and I could see the men bending over them and the bright flames in between the sticks of wood. Two men were carrying kettles of water, up from the river. Every detail of the camp was plainly visible, as if I had been standing on a bluff above the battlefield! It was as if I was looking down on the scene instead of being seated in my own yard and gazing into the sky . . . I called upon my children and one of my hired men to come and witness the spooky apparition while it lasted . . . we all stared into the skies in breathless silence . . . The wonderful picture hung in the sky for fifteen or twenty minutes, only seeming to flicker or tremble a moment or two at a time, and it faded away so gradually that it was hard to tell when the cloud ceased to be the picture. Or the picture ceased to be the cloud!

Christopher Allen Brewer is a native of the Oglala Sioux Nation, and his ancestors fought in the Battle of Little Big Horn. He and his partner, James Manda, have a paranormal investigation team known as Future Ghost, and they've been featured on the Biography Channel on their series, *My Ghost Story*. Brewer believes that the battlefield at Little Big Horn remains actively haunted, because violence always leaves a psychic imprint that lingers long after the traumatic event occurred, and he added, "The battlefield is a 'living area,' by which it is alive with spirit—like how in *Star Wars* they talk about areas rich with the dark side or light side of the force. Believe me, that battle will replay for centuries and I thank you for talking about it. Awareness is crucial to its healing."

So, perhaps the battlefield at Little Big Horn is still healing. Apparently, the big sky over Montana is suspended under an ancient, supernatural spell, inspired by the sacred sun dance, long ago. And some say that these ethereal, grand-scale illusions are why the state of Montana eventually became known as Spooky Sky Country.

HELL'S BELLS OF CHEYENNE

Death is a cruel mistress.

—James Bolton

Have you ever wondered how Cheyenne, Wyoming, became known as the magic city on the Plains? A published letter proved that it all began on Christmas Eve 1888, when carolers were huddled on boardwalks as busied street vendors peddled hot spiced wassail and roasted chestnuts. Jack Frost nipped at red noses as buckets of coal sold like hotcakes. Meanwhile, a familiar stranger limped into a local watering hole with a worried look in his eyes. But the affable saloon owner didn't take notice and shouted over a joyous crowd, "Look what the cat just dragged in . . . again!"

Crazy-eyed Jimmy nodded his head in nervous greeting and hastily hung his hat by the door. A potbellied stove crackled in the center of the room. Even more inviting was lovely Lily, who entertained a half-dozen barflies by taking talent on the player piano, and she looked especially fetching in a festive red holiday dress. After bellying up to the bar, Jimmy ordered a round for the house and watched Lily from afar, like an outcast wallflower. She smiled, and his heart died a thousand deaths. Jimmy secretly hoped that if he ever got the cooties that they'd be from Lily. Once her glass was empty, Lily sauntered across the floor and snuggled up to Jimmy with hot breath, hinting she was still thirsty.

With an obvious lisp, the mule skinner quickly stammered, "Merry Chrithmath, Lily my love . . . No time to exthplain, but I'm a dead man . . . stho, if you're still sthinking, I'm still buying!"

Around this time, a big fella called Lily a drunken harlot, and, desiring to defend her honor, the chivalrous mule skinner shouted that he had a "thotgun" at home, and he was determined to defend the "drunken harlot's" honor. But the bartender snuck up behind the mule skinner and walloped his head with a pistol butt. Poor Jimmy fell and fell hard, first hitting his noggin on the potbellied stove before planting his mug on the floor. Everyone laughed at the resounding thud—

except for Jimmy. So, his so-called friends assumed he was playing possum. One of them poured more beer down his throat while another propped him up in front of a player piano. Dancing, ringing handbells, and clanging spoons on bottles, the revelers sang fractured Christmas carols. Song requests were shouted over the cacophony. When Jimmy didn't respond, the saloonkeeper teased that maybe he couldn't hear, since blood was leaking from both his ears. And so the spoilsport was deemed unfit to play and was dragged into a backroom to recuperate. Meanwhile the band played like there was no tomorrow.

A few hours later, Lily went to check on her wayward Romeo and soon realized that the party was over. Jimmy the deadbeat was deader than a coffin nail. So, everyone piled into the paddy wagon and they were carted off to the pokey. Everyone except Jimmy, who spent the rest of Christmas Eve stiffening at the city morgue. While preparing Jimmy's body for burial, the coroner discovered a mysterious letter tucked inside his vest pocket, which read:

Dear Coroner,

I've taken the liberty of preparing my last will and testament in advance for good reason. Please allow me to explain . . . The beginning of my end came on the Eve of Christmas. I had a drink at the saloon and began walking home just as the sun was sinking over the horizon. Suddenly, I heard the glad call of Christmas bells, or so I thought . . . But the happy clanging soon turned hideous—mournful woes as terrible as those described by the bizarre pen of Dante about a hellish inferno. This strange cacophony seemingly came from the Saint Mark's Church. But the sanctuary was dark.

I considered running to the sheriff but changed my mind after recalling an old ghost story. It began with two Swedish stone masons who were hired to build the church bell tower. On Christmas Eve, they were working side by side, high on a scaffolding, when they began hearing the mournful tolling of a bell. But the new church bell was still housed in a shipping crate! The terrifying distraction caused one of the stone masons to fall. The other Swede worried about being deported, and so he sealed his partner's broken body inside the tower walls, although his buddy was still alive! Hastily, the coward then left Cheyenne, before anyone could discover his deceit. Not long after, terrible cries of sorrow were heard coming from the tower, and the carillon bell would boom on its own accord. In order to appease the Swede's ghost, a special room was built inside the bell tower, and this chamber of chillers was dedicated to the paranormal prisoner. The so-called Ghost Chamber boasted stained glass windows and a crystal chandelier, which hung from the tin print ceiling. But building a special room did nothing to placate the angry spirit, and the horrible hauntings continued. Night after night, terrible outcries and clanging bells continued. Surely, the dark secrets of Usher's House pale in comparison to those of Saint Mark's! . . .

So, I ran until I could run no more and ended up on Capitol Avenue with a twisted ankle. Adding insult to injury, I again heard the horrible sounds. Only this time the bells rang a gentler, softer tune, and the cries were from a mournful woman. These unsettling, passing waves would grow louder and then subside like a whimpering baby. It was terribly eerie. Christmas carolers and last-minute shoppers scattered like flies. Sales clerks were also visibly shaken, and they shuttered windows and locked doors. A posse of lawmen combed the streets, as I rested my swollen ankle upon a park bench and watched with morbid curiosity. But they found nothing to explain the mysterious din. A block later, I limped into my favorite saloon seeking comfort . . . lovely Lily was entertaining the crowd on the player piano, while the saloonkeeper shared spooky ghost stories.

I learned a new tale about the Banshee of Cheyenne. Although few folks had ever seen her face, her haunting screams were well known throughout the cow town. I then staggered outside for a smoke and hoped to calm my nerves. It was so quiet that you could have heard paint peel. Suddenly, the jingling of bells drew my eyes toward a shadowy wagon coming from around the corner. It was the coach of death! I had no time to hide. So, I just stood wide eyed with teeth chattering! A strange electricity in the air made my hair stand on end! As the dark coach drew closer it seemed to glow with a deep, purple haze under pale moonlight. Black flags and feather plumes streamed behind the hearse as the clip-clop of horseshoes echoed throughout shadowy streets. Pulling the carriage were six black stallions, and they were headless! The coachman, a grinning skeleton, wore nothing but a top hat and haunting smile. Wicked winds played eerie melodies as they whistled through his naked ribs. In one bony fist, the helmsmen held shimmering reins and in the other was a glistening silver handbell, which rang in step with the clicking horseshoes. As the hearse glided by, it was close enough to touch, and that's when I realized it was floating on air! I glanced through lacy windows and saw a woman in black lift a thin veil, revealing the most hideous face I'd ever seen! Hungry worms slithered from vacant eye sockets and she smiled with toothless gums. She pressed that hideous face against the glass pane and shrieked: "JIMMY . . . I WANT YOU!"

So, I bolted down the street like a jackrabbit and scuttled into my cabin, locking the door safely behind me. But I knew that no lock would keep death from my door. I'd heard the tolling of hell's bells, and a wicked banshee had called for me. My number was up, and this I knew.

So, I wrote this letter to you, dear coroner. Held within this envelope is money to settle my bar tab and for my proper burial. Whatever is left, you may have for your trouble. I'd like to thank you kindly for helping a dead man rest in peace. But please remember my fate and consider yours. Whenever the shades of evening fall over Cheyenne, know that mournful cries and the tolling of hell's bells warn of death's calling. And if the banshee's beckoning is heard, duck and hide! Otherwise you'll be joining me in the underworld of Lakeview Cemetery. Death is a cruel mistress, especially when she comes calling on holiday.

Merry Christmas to you and yours,

James Bolton

Shortly after this mysterious letter was published, the magic city on the Plains became a meeting place for ghost hunters and spiritualists, and if it weren't for Jimmy's letter, nobody would remember why!

SALTY GHOST OF SALT LAKE

He who commits injustice is ever made more
wretched than he who suffers it.

—Plato

A salty ghost haunts the Salt Lake City Cemetery. Legends about the paranormal potty mouth began long ago, when a teenaged couple raced into the Salt Lake City police station and asked to file a complaint against a haunted graveyard. Shivering and out of breath, the young man stammered:

> We . . . we . . . we've heard and seen a ghost . . . he was walking amongst the graves of City Cemetery . . . tall . . . thin . . . balding . . . wearing a flowing white funeral shroud. In one hand he held a swinging a lantern . . . in the other . . . he carried a shovel."

Wide eyed, the girl stammered:

> Yes . . . I saw him too . . . Holy Moly . . . was he ever cussing up a storm! I've never heard such salty language in my life!

Chief Smith was a practical fellow who didn't believe in the supernatural. But he knew that something funny had to be going on; otherwise he wouldn't be getting so many complaints about ghosts haunting the graveyard. So, the chief and his deputy went to the cemetery to investigate.

The undertaker, Mr. John Baptiste, welcomed them inside the caretaker's cottage. Soft spoken, John Baptiste was known around town as a spiffy dresser, and on this occasion the lanky bachelor was wearing a smart black suit and shiny new shoes. A class ring hugged his pinky finger, and a diamond stickpin winked from a satin lapel. After Chief Smith shared the teenagers' frightful account, Mr. Baptiste used a bony finger to push wire-framed spectacles to the bridge of his nose and demurred, "With all due respect officer, these are hallowed grounds . . .

John Baptiste still haunts
the Salt Lake City Cemetery.
Author's Collection.

we have signs posted against trespassing after dark. I believe that ghost hunting is a distasteful and frivolous affair. It's also dangerous. Someone could trip over a tombstone and hurt themselves. So, if I ever catch those meddling kids around here after hours, I will not hesitate in pressing charges against those miserable miscreants."

The next morning, Chief Smith had even more trouble dished onto his proverbial plate. Reports were that the Utah territorial governor had tried to get frisky with a pretty Mormon widow. So she belted him with a frying pan, and the randy politician made a hasty escape, as an angry mob followed in hot pursuit. Once the Mormon militia caught up with the governor, they tied him to a cottonwood and plucked a nugget from his Fruit of the Looms. Adding insult to injury, they called him nutty names and mocked his impaired condition. But the fun and games didn't last for long. At the Salt Lake City Jail, Chief Smith charged the rebels with article A-1: criminal amputation of a politician's left testicle. While awaiting trial, Moroni Clawson attempted a daring jailbreak. But a guardsman shot him dead, and the rebel was buried in Pauper's Field.

One month later, Clawson's clan caught wind of his failed escape, and they requested to have him reburied in their family plot. But when Moroni's corpse was exhumed, he was found without a proper coffin, and he was as naked as a newborn! Chief Smith ordered a prompt investigation and was surprised to find that hundreds of graves had been robbed! So, Chief Smith and his deputy took their findings to the home of John Baptiste.

When the misanthrope opened the door to the caretaker's cottage, he was wearing a smart azure smoking jacket with matching silk ascot. Smith pardoned their intrusion and joked, "Do morticians always dress to kill?" Baptiste smiled and demurred, "Please make yourself at home boys, and I'll be back in a jiffy."

The cluttered parlor held fine furniture and dainty flower arrangements, but it ranked of mothballs and death. A few moments later, Mr. Baptiste sashayed back into the room carrying a silver serving tray, saying, "Please help yourself to burgundy and liver pâté whilst I light the candelabra atop the pipe organ . . . any song requests?"

"FREE BIRD!" squawked a black raven from a gilded cage.

46

Obviously annoyed, Mr. Baptiste turned beet red and bellowed, "Silence, Edgar! Nobody asked for your bird- brained opinion!" In a fit of anger, Baptiste stood up from the organ bench and marched over to throw a red velvet drape over the distraction.

But Edgar rattled his cage in defiance and screeched a beak full of fowl language by squawking: "I'm an eagle! Pearls! Diamonds! Furs!"

Meanwhile, Chief Smith recognized Mr. Baptiste's shiny, new shoes as belonging to a dead man—Mr. Moroni Clawson! The lawman grilled the gravedigger, and, at first, Baptiste denied everything.

But finally, he broke down and sniffled, "Okay, I confess to borrowing Clawson's leather oxfords. And yes, it was me and my big-mouthed bird, out robbing the dead after dark. I wore a funeral shroud to scare off trespassers. But being an undertaker is awfully hard work, and since this profession doesn't pay dirt, most of us have gone to digging up fringe benefits, like what I'd harvested from the grave of Mr. Moroni Clawson. It would be a crying shame to see such fine garments wither away on rotting flesh—"waste not want not" is my motto. Many of the coffins I converted into fine furniture or chopped up and sold as polished firewood. I made a veritable fortune by selling brass and silver casket fixtures to the foundry. I sold most of the clothing to resale shops, but I took my fair share of the easy pickings. This fine smoking jacket I borrowed from our former mayor—God rest his soul. And I recycled hundreds of burial shrouds and underwear, which I stretched, painted, and converted into window treatments and lampshades."

The following morning, the remaining stash of stolen jewelry, dresses, shirts, trousers, coats, shoes, and underwear were spread in the main hall of the county courthouse. Newspapers across the country reported about the horrific scandal. On March 1, 1862, the *Philadelphia Inquirer* lamented:

A more heart rendering spectacle can't be imagined . . . Funeral shrouds and winding sheets for young and old, male and female, some torn while removing them from stiffening corpses were strewn about the room . . . It was a sad sight to see anxious mothers seeking for, yet dreading to find, the little garment, torn with rude inhuman hands from their infant darlings, whom they had laid away in the tomb, never dreaming they'd be disturbed until their sleeping dust should be quickened by resurrecting angels . . . Twas a sad, sad scene, from which we were happy to turn away . . . a heavy gloom like a dark pall hangs over the city . . . sorrow has entered anew into every household. The cemetery is being visited by crowds . . . although weather is cold and stormy. The rich man in his carriage, the poor man on foot, the young widow, the staid matron, the old and infirm who have lost friends to death, seem to have an ardent desire to visit the desecrated graves . . .

Angry citizens urged the Lynch Code. But the mayor retorted that the stinky situation would be dealt with through proper law and order. Meanwhile, a raging crowd grew outside the caretaker's cottage, and the chief of police worried that there'd be trouble.

"Stone him!" screamed a young mother, holding a torn baby blanket, and Edger squawked, "Feed him to the lions!"

Ironically these callous suggestions gave Chief Smith an ingenious idea. So, he ordered Baptiste to pack his bags, and then late that night the prisoner was smuggled away from the caretaker's cottage. By the light of a knowing moon, they rowed across the inhospitable waters of Salt Lake until docking upon a remote island. The undertaker was ordered to kneel on bended knees, remove his hat, and lay his head upon a tree stump. The steel blade of an angry saber glistened in silent moonlight as it was produced from a cool, leather sheath. Baptiste sobbed for mercy as the weapon was raised high. And then in a heartbeat, Baptiste's ears went sailing over ripples of Salt Lake! Adding insult to injury, his forehead was tattooed with the words "CROPPED FOR ROBBING THE DEAD!" Mr. Baptiste was given a sack of dry beans, a jug of drinking water, and his only friend, Edgar. Then Chief Smith cleared his throat and bellowed, "The philosopher Plato once said, 'He who commits injustice is ever made more wretched than he who suffers it.' But you have shown little remorse for the unethical acts you have committed against your fellow man. Mr. John Baptiste, in the eyes of God and the pious citizens of Salt Lake City, you have exhibited some treacherous traits, that we as a community feel are unwholesome and unwelcome. You are a greedy, despicable, uncivilized clod . . . If I could stone you or throw you to the lions, I surely would. But instead, you are being exiled to Antelope Island, to fend for yourself against other wild animals, such as yourself . . . may God have mercy upon your wicked soul."

Baptiste began sobbing like a baby, and Edgar squawked "Nevermore!"

A year later, Chief Smith returned to Antelope Island. Built into the cove, he discovered a grass hut and hoisted above the roof was a white flag made from underwear. But John Baptiste and his bird-brained companion were nowhere to be found. Years later, an earless John Baptiste was spotted in the Salt Lake City Cemetery. He was also recognized by his tattooed forehead and unruly raven. But the former undertaker had a peculiar glow about his person. Rumors swirled that Baptiste had returned from the dead!

Over the years, the hauntings continued. One newspaper report told that thirty cars went to the cemetery on a full-moon night, and how over fifty witnesses saw balls of lights bouncing throughout the graveyard!

Even today, old timers claim that the old boneyard is haunted. On nights of the full moon, John Baptiste can be seen floating around the cemetery. His ethereal presence glows in the moonlight as he swings a trusty lantern. On his shoulder rides a black raven that can be heard cussing up a storm. Edgar is still recognized by his salty talk, and that's why he's become known as the Salty Ghost of Salt Lake!

WITCH OF THE DIABLO MOUNTAINS

Be Careful What You Wish For!

— W. W. Jacobs from "Tale of the Monkey's Paw"

"Diablo" is Spanish for "devil." So, it might make you wonder why a mountain range was named after evil incarnate. Old timers claim the diablos were christened after the devilish cries that have long echoed throughput those mighty monarchs. And now you'll learn how this spooky legend all began . . .

Long ago, in the Diablo Mountains, there lived a Castilian nobleman who loved nothing more than the song of birds. He kept many as treasured pets in a special aviary. One lovely morning he went hunting for songbirds to add to his collection. In the center of an alpine forest was a peaceful spring where many creatures went for drink, and it was his favorite place for bird watching. The nobleman enjoyed a welcoming swim in the shimmering waters and then spread a picnic blanket under a shady tree. While enjoying his lunch, red-breasted robins, steel-blue tomtits, and gay finches fluttered about, all singing glad song. When suddenly, from mortal lips he heard sweet singing. And then from behind a waterfall came a young Indian maiden with long, black braids. She carried an earthen jug of water, which she joyfully filled from the spring. Her lovely voice was as clear as a bell, but she was homely and plain looking. Blissfully, the nobleman listened and was no longer angry that she'd frightened away the chorale of songbirds. Unaware that he was watching her, the songstress was startled when he began clapping for an encore. The maiden turned in embarrassment and was about to run away, until the Castilian beckoned her to stay by demurring, "Dear lady, forgive my silent intrusion; I was just enjoying your happy song. Please, fill my goblet from your jug."

As he took a long draft from its cooling contents, she sheepishly raised her brown eyes. His was the first face she could find no fault with. It was as if

Adonis had fallen from the heavens and was standing before her. He smiled and she died a thousand deaths. Then he patted her head, like a puppy, before riding off into the sunset. With an unfaltering gaze she faithfully followed his leave until she saw him no more. Longing to be with him, the dreamy teenager sighed aloud: "Ah, if only I were a real songbird . . . perhaps the handsome stranger would catch me in his net and take me back to his fancy home. I wish I could be his to keep. I'd be a happy prisoner, as I should see him every day."

Suddenly, an old woman appeared from nowhere. Dressed in a raggedy black dress, her long white hair was tangled with cobwebs. One eye was covered by a black patch, and the other bulged from its socket, as if it were trying to escape from the hideous face it clung from. Making matters worse, she smelled like dirty socks. Suddenly, the witch croaked, "What's that I hear? You'd like to be a real songbird? Be careful what you wish for, sweet maid." The old woman cackled and hissed, "I can make your dreams come true, for I am a great and powerful witch! With my help, you shall be a pretty bird with dazzling feathers! Your bewitching beauty and happy song shall be highly praised and admired by all! And the man you desire will love you and forsake all others! But my gift comes with a price. Once the nobleman falls asleep each night, you must fly back to my cave and be my slave until sunrise. And if you don't return to me by midnight, you shall pay with your life! Will you agree to my simple plan?"

"Yes, yes, yes!" the homely maiden enthusiastically replied.

"Then follow me, and I will give you a drop of powerful love potion." And with these few words, the gleeful girl followed the old witch to her nearby cave.

The next day, the nobleman returned to the spring with bird net in hand. The maiden was secretly hiding, and upon seeing the nobleman, she willingly flew into his net.

On his way home, he listened happily to her joyful songs and cooed, "Such an easy catch! You are the most beautiful creature I have ever seen, and your sweet song is the prettiest I've ever heard . . . My many other pets pale in comparison. From this day forward, I shall keep only you! You shall be my one and only beloved!"

Over time, the young noblemen's love grew for his treasured bird. From sunrise to sunset, the maiden perched upon his shoulder and sang glad songs. After the nobleman would fall asleep at night, she would linger for a few moments at his bedside, longing to be his lover. But duty called. So, she'd stretch her wings and take flight to the witch's cave, where the old woman would turn her back into a peasant girl. All night long the maiden cooked and cleaned while the witch lounged about like queen of the castle. Upon the first cock-a-doodle-do of a rooster, the unhappy prisoner would fly back to her gilded cage.

Then one fateful day, the nobleman announced that it was time for him to marry. His intended bride and her hefty dowry would soon be arriving from Spain. There was laid a bountiful feast, and guests came from all over the countryside. The celebration went well into the night, as the maiden patiently waited for her master's return. She worried that the witch would be angry. She pulled at her feathers and fretted by rattling her golden cage.

Eventually the nobleman began missing his prized songbird. So he went to fetch her, thinking she'd gleefully entertain his wedding guests. But the jealous songbird ducked head under wing and refused to sing. Bewildered by her cruel rejection, the nobleman began petting her, and then he kissed her for the first time. Happily the songbird beat her wings and lifted her sweet voice.

But the beautiful bride became a green-eyed monster. Overwhelmed with jealousy, she desired nothing more than death for her fine-feathered rival! The envious bride wrapped her arms around her husband and squealed, "I wish for this fine bird to keep in my chambers, where I shall cherish its sweet song!"

Wanting to please his new wife, the nobleman purred "My only wish is to make you happy. If you will love her as much as I do, then she's yours."

But the songbird knew the bride had a dark heart. So, she burst free from her gilded cage and took flight over the wedding party. Startled guests jumped over tables and chairs, trying to catch the crafty beauty. The exhausting chase lasted until the clock struck midnight, and then the renegade songbird gently fluttered to the floor, like a deflated balloon.

Suddenly, a strange mist hovered over the entire scene, and a sleeping girl appeared where the bird had fallen. Wedding guests gasped in disbelief and the nobleman's mother shrieked, "Something wicked this way comes! That lovely songbird was nothing but an evil enchantress! She's bewitched my son with satanic arts! Throw her onto the fire! Quickly, before the she-devil awakens!"

And with that hasty demand, the sleeping woman was thrown onto the fire! Ear-piercing screams and the stench of burnt feathers scattered wedding guests like flies! Jealousy and murder most foul had forever changed the landscape, because every midnight thereafter, the maiden's haunting screams shattered tranquility for as far as the crow flies!

And so it was that these mighty monarchs became known as the haunted diablos. And even after all these years, this cautionary tale still serves as an everlasting reminder that we should all be more careful about what we wish for, especially in the devilish Diablo Mountains.

TRUTH OF OLD MAN MOUNTAIN

Hell is truth seen too late.

—Thomas Hobbes

The adventures of *Alice in Wonderland* or *Rip Van Winkle* pale in comparison to the inexplicable journey that made the Boyd party famous. Colonel Joseph T. Boyd was the founding father of Golden and Colorado state secretary. As an educated engineer, he was hired to investigate a rugged area that would one day be known as Rocky Mountain National Park. The Denver & Rio Grande Railroad paid for the land survey because they'd planned a new route through the region. So, in August 1885, Boyd, along with three of his esteemed colleagues, rode toward the towering inspiration of Long's Peak. After a long day's ride, they set up camp. But it rained all night, and so they didn't get to enjoy the breathtaking view. The next morning, their soggy gear was packed, and the party continued their treacherous journey. Around noon it stopped raining, but it was still colder than a knot on the North Pole.

As their horses clopped along a narrow ridge, Boyd leaned back in his saddle and shouted over his shoulder, saying, "Do you all see the blue mists snaking over those yonder cliffs? Well, my friends, the natives feared that smoky haze as being the breath of a man-eating serpent! In fact, whenever they saw the blue mists rolling into the Saint Vrain Valley, they'd grab talismans and shake medicine rattles to divert evil spirits. Late at night the so-called blue serpent would slither into wigwams and steal away with children. As a man of science, I've never taken to superstitious beliefs. But I guess some folks are dumber than dirt!"

Onward they trudged through the mud until stumbling upon the exact spot where they'd camped the night before. In a sudden fit of anger, Boyd jumped from his horse, stomped on his hat, and chastised Sergeant Pierce for getting them lost. "By golly, I thought of you as an expert navigator, until now," Boyd admonished.

The Boyd party traveled through a time warp,
which aged their appearance and broadened their minds.
Author's Collection.

Sheepishly, Pierce retrieved a compass from his saddlebag. The needle began spinning counterclockwise and never rested on true north. Bewildered, the foursome stared at the bewitched instrument with wide eyes, as they trembled in fear. An unseen force rippled through the air, and the hair on the back of their necks stood at attention.

Colonel Boyd insisted that there must be a reasonable explanation, and deducted that certain pockets in the landscape possessed magnetic anomalies. "The boys back home will never believe this strange story," he said with an uneasy chuckle.

The following morning, the eager adventurists came upon a mountain that had once been sanctuary to the Utes, Cheyenne, and Arapahoe Indians. At the base of the mighty monolith stood a huge rock formation that resembled two human heads with menacing eyes. One of the spooky stone sentinels gazed wickedly to the south while the other slit-eyed giant glared to the north. Sargent Pierce wanted to sketch the intriguing monument, but Colonel Boyd insisted that they keep moving.

Upon reaching an enchanting meadow, they stopped for lunch. Scattered about the field of colorful wildflowers were mysterious mounds of stacked rocks. Piles contained chunks of sky-blue and green turquoise along with glistening smoky-brown quartz and brilliant amethyst crystals. Radiant rose quartz and iridescent moonstone sparkled in abundance. A surprising array of seashells adorned one impressive mound. Obviously, some of these geological specimens had come from distant lands.

An amateur anthropologist, Boyd offered his astute opinion: "We may have trespassed through an ancient Indian burial grounds. I once read how the natives brought a token rock from their homelands as a gift, whenever they would visit the distant graves of mighty chieftains. Burial mounds held great hoodoo, and anyone who trespassed upon sacred ground would suffer . . . that is, if you believe in ancient Indian curses!" Boyd chuckled at the absurd legend. Then he scrambled to the top of a rock pile, where he enjoyed the view with a juicy, red apple.

After dining with the dead, Boyd and his merry men followed a well-worn Indian path. A towering rock wall seemed impregnable until they discovered a hidden aperture behind a large boulder. The colonel reasoned that the keyhole might lead into a natural tunnel, which might save the railroad time and money dynamiting. So, they retrieved a lantern, packed provisions, and tethered their horses to a nearby tree. After squeezing through the tight entrance, they stood for a moment, allowing their pupils to adjust to the dim light. Black carbon had tarnished the stone ceiling. Boyd recognized the soot as torchlight stains and realized that they were inside a secret passageway. In the distance they noticed a speck of light, and as they shuffled down the narrow corridor, the slight glimmer grew into a welcoming rush of sunshine. Much to their astonishment they were welcomed by a lush, tropical paradise! Succulently sweet, warm air was heavy with the alluring aroma of jasmine and honeysuckle. The colorful landscape was abundant with exotic plants and wildlife. Boyd couldn't believe his eyes upon recognizing a blue-footed booby and wondered how the South American bird species had found its way into the Rockies. Yet, there were two of them, fighting over a red banana! Sargent Pierce joked that they'd gone through hell and had accidentally stumbled upon paradise!

Boyd saw dollar signs and suggested a partnership where they'd develop the land into a resort to be called the Garden of Eden. And then, into the garden a serpent did come . . . a colossal, blue snake slithered down the trunk of an apple tree, as the pounding of distant tribal drums quickened hearts. The colonel beckoned for his associates to follow the serpent, which headed straight toward the hypnotic sound . . . *BOOMBA* . . . *BOOMBA* . . . *BOOMBA*. The yellow-eyed viper led them over a clear-running stream . . . *BOOMBA* . . . *BOOMBA* . . . *BOOMBA* . . . and into thick shrubbery . . . *BOOMBA* . . . *BOOMBA* . . . *BOOM-BA*, where they discovered the entrance to a hidden cave. As if entranced, the men dropped to their knees and slithered into the hole after the blue demon. But the snake disappeared into thin air, just as the drum beat faded . . . *boomba* . . . *boomba* . . . *boomba*. Suddenly, they were enveloped in a cool blanket of darkness. But then the terrible silence was shattered by spine-tingling whispers, followed by painful groans, hysterical wailing, and hideous shrieks of laughter! In haste, the foursome crawled forward as if compelled by an unseen force, until they fumbled upon a large chamber. This immense cavern was illuminated by a strange, ethereal light. In the center of the room, a mound of twinkling treasure was surrounded by dozens of human skeletons!

Colonel Boyd assessed the situation and ascertained that they'd accidentally stumbled into an ancient burial chamber belonging to a great Aztec chieftain! But as he eagerly reached for a nifty souvenir, the earth's rumbling shook the cavern, and blinding light assaulted from every direction. This insult was accompanied by an agonizing cacophony! Invisible legions jabbered in archaic, guttural languages, which Boyd and his men somehow understood. Ancient, esoteric wisdom relayed about other dimensions . . . history . . . the future . . . time and space, folded into one grand masterpiece, and they were dizzied by the immaculate whirl!

A thunderous clap rallied their attention, and a deep, guttural voice trumpeted over the terrifying din: "DEATH COMES TO THOSE WHO TREAD UPON HALLOWED GROUNDS!"

Turning on heels, the party fumbled back through the harrowing darkness, as wicked laughter chased their rapid footfalls. Upon stumbling from the secret keyhole, they realized that a dense, blue mist had enveloped Old Man Mountain, and their horses had vanished! As the party silently trudged back to camp, they couldn't see anything but smothering blue mists. And following at their heels were inhumane screams, growls, and wicked laughter! Once Boyd reached camp, he turned to see that his comrades had vanished!

Days later, Colonel Boyd's men finally stumbled into camp. And just like Boyd, they'd inexplicably aged many years—with long, white beards and their chiseled faces resembling shriveled prunes. Newspapers featured interviews with members of the Boyd party, which showed before-and-after photographs of the formerly youthful explorers. Newsmen from coast to coast covered the amazing story, and the public was captivated. And so it was that the Boyd campsite became suitably known as Old Man Mountain.

For many years thereafter, Boyd searched but never rediscovered paradise lost. Memory about the profound journey through the secret passageway served as quiet consolation. But until his dying day, Boyd swore the story was true. Alas, if hell was truth seen too late, then perhaps they'd seen heaven!

GHOSTLY LOVERS OF VIRGINIA CITY

Love is blind, and lovers cannot see the pretty follies
that they themselves commit.

—William Shakespeare

Love is blind. Especially in Virginia City, where two soulmates haunt an entire ghost town! This sappy saga began over a century ago, when a gunslinger known as Jack Slade met the love of his life, Virginia Dale. Although as opposite as night and day, dime store novels would later recall how their love began at first sight. They'd met when Virginia was a fallen flower from a garden with many beds. And from a poor family, she'd always desired nothing more than the finer things in life, such as silk kimonos, flashy rings, and fine toilet water with Italian names. She was a timeless beauty, the kind you'd see smiling from a calendar page.

Jack Slade was quite different: a simple man, short and scrappy, with a face that only a mother could love—especially since he had three ears. The smallest was always worn in his vest pocket and had once belonged to a sworn enemy. Jack believed the vile trophy protected him against other back-stabbing friends who'd turned foe. Yes, Jack Slade went everywhere with his petrified ear fob, and with his wife, Virginia Dale, and with a stubborn donkey he'd fondly named Brother Brutus.

Virginia was a good influence on Jack, but Brother Brutus was not. Because whenever Jack got into trouble, he'd always blame Brother Brutus. Finally, Virginia had had enough of their drunken shenanigans, saying she'd leave them both for good if they didn't strive for higher ground. And so it was that the Slades decided to turn over a new leaf in the mountains of Montana Territory, where Jack and Brother Brutus landed lucrative jobs as toll road guardians.

In the beginning, everything was hunky-dory for the Slade family. Jack built a rock cottage for his wife and a barn for his best friend. The Slade homestead was located next to the toll booth along the main road into Virginia City. Mrs. Slade was honored to have the nearby town named after her, because she was

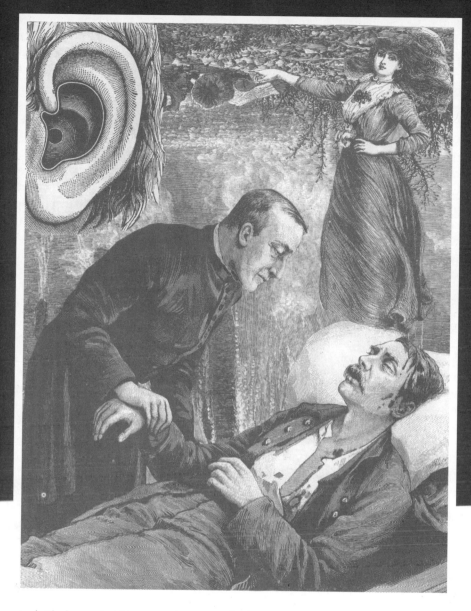

Jack Slade carried his enemy's mummified ear in his vest pocket for good luck.
Author's Collection.

said to be the prettiest gal around. Brother Brutus enjoyed munching in greener pastures, and Jack was asked to join an exclusive vigilante gang known as the 777 Club. Jack went to club meetings in Virginia City, paid his dues, and presented himself as a pious member of the community. Brother Brutus did his business only outside city limits, and Jack always used a pooper scooper.

But it wasn't long before Jack and Brother Brutus went down a dark road and ruined their halcyon dreams of being respectable citizens. This happened one stormy night at the Bloody Knuckle Saloon, when Jack boasted of being mighty thirsty and wanting to trade a "beer for an ear." Then he tossed his petrified human ear fob on the bar top and laughed like a hyena. But on this regrettable occasion, Jack was the only one laughing except for Brother Brutus, who hee-hawed at the witticism. And when the saloonkeeper refused the mummified trophy, he soon regretted hasty words. Jack got a bee in his bonnet and shot everything that wasn't moving, while Brother Brutus kicked up his heels and brayed. Adding insult to injury, Jack and Brother Brutus rode up to the mayor's pretty wife while she was watering her flower garden. Brutus gobbled daffodils without being invited to lunch, and Jack asked if she'd like to see his stiff organ. The mayor didn't think that the Slade brothers were very funny, and so he chased them from his yard with a booming shotgun!

Come morning, the hellions were still full of piss and vinegar . . . Jack ambushed a milk wagon and Brother Brutus drove it into a ravine. Hungry babes went without breakfast. Maddened moms stormed after the drunkards with pots, pans, and rolling pins, since they wanted to beat the living tarnation out of the miserable miscreants!

But Jack and Brother Brutus evaded the she-devils by ducking into the Chinese laundry. Once the coast was clear, Jack ran across the street, where he ripped the preacher's red long johns off a clothesline and dumped the clean load down the poop shoot of an outhouse! Meanwhile, Brother Brutus fertilized the preacher's lawn with recycled daffodils. At the livery, the dastardly duo released horses into the streets and brayed at the awful chaos they'd created.

After they attempted to kidnap the judge, it was the last straw—the avenging 777 Club captured the troublemakers and tossed them into the pokey. During their drunken stupor, Jack lost his lucky ear, and Brutus lost his taste for loose ladies and liquor. The next day, due legal process was lost to a mob's madness. Slade was dragged from the jailhouse, lassoed, hog-tied, and whipped without mercy.

Boastfully, the sheriff bellowed, "Pay attention folks, because this is what happens to drunkards in Virginia City," and Jack whimpered, "Something's rotten in Denmark . . . I thought you were friends . . . **Et tu, Brutus**?"

But Jack's loyal companion was nowhere to be found—he'd broken free from bondage and had escaped down the toll road in order to warn Virginia! Once at the rock cottage, Mrs. Slade jumped on the back of Brother Brutus and they rode into town together, Hell-bent for leather!

But revenge of the 777 Club was never served cold. Virginia and her brother-in-law arrived just in time to see Jack being cut down from the dirty noose. A cowardly crowd scattered as she fell onto her husband's warm corpse. The weary widow heaved with great sorrow as she covered Jack with salty tears and sweet kisses. And after licking Jack's red face with a purple tongue, Brutus brayed like there was no tomorrow! Alas, Jack Slade was buried before sundown in his wife's beloved flower garden, since she believed that having his grave within eyesight would be comforting.

But that night, Virginia was tortured by what she couldn't see . . . Jack's haunting screams begging for mercy! Night after night, the weary widow would be awakened by her husband's unmistakable, raspy voice calling from his garden grave . . . "Virginia, Virginia . . . Please save me!"

Eventually, the weary widow couldn't bear being separated from her soulmate. So, she paid top dollar to have Jack's coffin exhumed. His corpse was then sealed inside a premium, custom-made, zinc-lined coffin, and whiskey was poured over his body to preserve his remains. (Although from the way Jack drank, he was probably already pickled.) And then the grieving widow tossed a feather mattress over Jack's fancy casket, and she slept with her decaying hubby every night.

Thankfully, this desperate measure kept her troubling nightmares at bay. But the putrid odor soon grew unbearable. Come the first sign of spring, Jack's coffin was tethered to the top of a stagecoach and he was reburied in a distant town. Although Salt Lake City became his final, final resting place, some say Jack Slade has never rested in peace. Because legend tells that while walking down the dusty streets of Virginia City today, you can still hear the scrappy gunslinger crying out for his long, lost love, as he whimpers . . . "Virginia, Virginia . . . Please save me!"

And yet still another jackass also haunts the old ghost town. Night after night, a phantom donkey charges into Virginia City from the old toll road. And once the glowing apparition of Brother Brutus gets to the corral where Jack was executed, this loyal phantom suddenly disappears into the ether.

Although this ghost story may sound like a pile of donkey doo, it makes perfect sense to experts in such matters. Because if ever there was a man and beast cut from the same cloth, it would surely be Jack Slade and his shady steed. And so it goes that these soulmates are doomed to be separated throughout eternity. Love is blind, and perhaps that's why they can't find one another in the afterlife. And what better reason could there be for the Slade brothers to haunt an entire ghost town?

PHANTOM JOYRIDER OF PUEBLO

Keep your friendships in repair.

—Ralph Waldo Emerson

Few bonds are closer than those of fraternal brotherhoods, especially in a proud and loyal union town. At Pueblo's Hose Company Number 3 Firehouse Museum, jokes between friends have continued long after death. This strange tale begins with John F. Bishop. Determined to make a name for himself, the young architect jumped at the offer to design the new firehouse for Hose Company 3. "Johnny" was ambitious about the project, since he'd always wanted to leave his stamp on the burgeoning town of Pueblo. During the planning process, he'd made many new friends. In fact, after the firehouse was completed in 1895, he dropped by every Saturday evening to play checkers with the good ole boys. On occasion he'd volunteer his time out in the field if his brothers needed help. The handsome bachelor was also a member of the next-door Masonic temple. So, the lodge and firehouse became his home away from home.

Then on Saturday, August 7, 1904, Johnny didn't show up at the firehouse as expected. His rocking chair sat empty as the clock ticked minutes into hours. Around 10:00 p.m., the phone rang, and Chief Campbell answered to a dead line. This irritating intrusion happened several more times. But the captain just rolled his eyes and blamed a static phone line on foul weather. Two hours later, an emergency call came from the nearby farming community of Eden, just nine miles north of Pueblo. Once firefighters arrived on the scene, the crew discovered that a trestle bridge had collapsed over the Arkansas River, just as a train had crossed. Dozens of battered bodies littered the swollen riverbanks, and angry waters were still on the rise. Victims suffocated in the unrelenting quicksand, and more than a hundred men, women, and children drowned in frigid waters. Many of the corpses washed down the churning river of death, never to be found.

John F. Bishop was identified only by the engraved Masonic ring that he always wore on his left pinky finger. Sadly, the hook-and-ladder fire company didn't save a single living soul. The frazzled firemen returned to company head-quarters with heavy hearts and heads hung low. But a bright moment occurred when the chief discovered that during the night, Johnny's familiar rocking chair had flipped over, and his checkerboard had fallen onto the floor. Not a single word was spoken as the bewildered crew picked up scattered pieces.

After Johnny's funeral, the gang began dreaming about their deceased brother, and it seemed like he was attempting to give them a message from the great hereafter. Lo and behold, a federal investigation found that the Denver & Rio Grande Railroad was guilty of building an inferior bridge. Perhaps the architect's ghost was warning his friends about the possibility of a dangerous cover-up. Because the Eden train wreck was a senseless disaster that could have been easily prevented with practical planning. Yet, within days, still another hasty bridge was built and hurried trains roared once again through the freshly fertilized fields of Eden's despaired gardens.

Although the railroad company didn't show remorse, at least the president of the United States declared that the Eden train wreck was the worst disaster in American railroad history. Out of respect for Johnny, firemen wore black bands around their upper left arm and flew the flag at half mast. But this sincere gesture didn't placate Johnny's plaintive spirit. Because just as soon as the crew removed the mourning bands, the unsettling hauntings began with a barrage of mysterious phone calls tormenting the crew. Whenever anyone answered, all that could be heard was dead silence. Sometimes there was a familiar beeping noise, which sounded like an emergency signal in Morse code! And lights flickered every time Johnny's name was mentioned. Sometimes, his perky voice could be clearly heard on the main level, while the firemen were sleeping in the loft. But once the guys hollered out a nervous hello to their paranormal pal, his familiar chattering instantly ceased.

These spooky shenanigans became as regular as clockwork. The month of August was an active time for Johnny's restless spirit, since it was the anniversary of the Eden train accident. Then after two officers died in the line of duty. And so a wall in the firehouse was dedicated to fallen heroes. Inspired stories written about their selfless acts of courage were typed and framed beside stoic photographs.

One fateful day, a man's handprint appeared on the window next to the proud shrine. The left pinky finger looked as though it was wearing a wide band, just like the Masonic ring that John once wore. This window was washed, but the image reemerged. The glass pane was replaced, but the red stain returned, time after time.

The Old Grand Dame didn't lose her spirit or spirits after becoming a museum in 2002. Over the years, there have been many serious questions regarding the immense amount of paranormal activity witnessed at the Hose Company 3 Firehouse Museum. Two of the spookiest incidents are unexplainable . . . at 3:30 a.m., on March 21, 1964, the sleeping crew were jolted awake by a blaring fire alarm. After zipping down the shiny brass pole, the firemen found a bewildering

The old Hose Company Number 3 Firehouse Museum
is haunted by a phantom joyrider.
Author's Collection.

surprise: their fire truck had left the building without them! Everyone glanced around the garage and scratched their helmets in wonder. Eventually, the chief found their 1960 Seagraves fire truck. Sputtering out of gas, the driverless truck was stalled in the middle of Broadway Street. Apparently, the engine had started up by itself. Then the fire truck burst through the garage door and rolled out into the street. Somehow it avoided several passing cars until it drifted to a stop.

Police detectives and insurance investigators theorized that the truck was left in first gear and then rolled out the door. But this lame excuse didn't hold water. After all, how could the engine start without a living finger to turn the key in the ignition slot? Or, how did the engine have enough horsepower to burst through the doors, without a human foot punching pedal to the metal? This bizarre incident made all the newspapers, and these crazy stories only fueled rumors about the haunted firehouse. After that fateful night, the officers at Hose Company Number 3 earned their fair share of spooky bragging rights around the watercooler.

Exactly forty years later, the ghost driver rode again! On the morning of the annual firemen's banquet, three volunteers were at the firehouse loading vehicles with party provisions. A Model T Ford that once belonged to the first fire chief had become a permanent display at the museum, and it was to be driven to the nearby party. The vehicle had been converted from an old manual crank to a modern starter. Because of this crude conversion, it took each of the three men several attempts to get the stubborn engine to turn over. But once she got the cobwebs out of her bonnet, she purred like a kitten. One of the volunteers took the old gal for a quick spin. After circling the block, he left her idling in the back parking lot in order to keep the engine charged. But before the trio finished packing their vehicles, the Model T left for the party without them!

The driverless Ford was first spotted by a woman who lived across the street from the back parking lot. Upon observing the driverless, runaway car, she ran into the street and screamed at the weaving jalopy. But it did little good, because driverless Fords won't ever listen. As the renegade was headed straight for the woman's parked van, she sprayed the vehicle with a garden hose while shouting "SCAT!" Apparently, this gesture got the car's attention, because it made a sudden U-turn behind the parking lot of Davis Mortuary and then maneuvered through a half-dozen grimacing tombstones! At Evans Street, the Model T made a right-hand turn and nearly ran over a drop-jawed pedestrian. Stunned witnesses flew toward the car, flapping their arms like a flock of seagulls. But the Ford just reared its horses and galloped down Evans Street, at the breakneck speed of five miles per hour. At Broadway Street, the floundering Ford took a rolling right turn, but at least the blinker was used during that sudden maneuver. Two hundred yards later, the jalopy jolted to the right and crashed into the curb, which brought the phantom's joyride to a sputtering halt. The fire chief heard a loud engine rumbling in front of the building. Imagine his surprise upon looking out the window and seeing the Model T idling, without a driver! Again the police and press soon followed. But a plausible explanation for the phantom driver of Hose Company Number 3 Firehouse has never been found.

Few bonds are tighter than those of fraternal brotherhood, and so it seems that Johnny's ghost is still connected to his former home away from home.

BANSHEE BRIDE OF BOOT HILL

Heav'n has no rage, like love to hatred turn'd,
nor Hell a fury, like a woman scorn'd.

—William Congreve, *The Mourning Bride*

Only the sick and old die in bed while resting in peace. Yet, there's one pioneer cemetery where everyone buried there died in bed while making love. So, it's no wonder this old graveyard seems more haunted than most.

Let us begin with a nerdy bookkeeper by the name of Mr. King. Short, bald, and plump, Mr. King was the nervous sort of fellow with a perpetually damp forehead. Also making him sweat was his much-younger wife. He'd met the bashful beauty through a mail order catalog for lonely hearted Yanks seeking British brides. A broken-winged dove, Agnes Elizabeth was thrice widowed and without children. So the lifelong bachelor beckoned her to join him stateside. At the Franklin Boarding House, the downtrodden newlyweds became acquainted with the founding father of Bonanza City, Mr. Charles Franklin.

A shrewd real-estate developer, Charles took pity upon his fellow Englishmen by giving Mr. King a job as a traveling sales agent. And during Mr. King's absence, Mr. Franklin enjoyed tea for two with the English Rose. Then one fateful day, while Mr. Franklin and Mrs. King sat sipping Earl Grey over Emily Brontë, the doorbell rang. Mr. King had arrived home earlier than expected, riding in a hearse! Shot through the heart while making love to another man's wife. Being a gentleman, Mr. Franklin paid for the funeral and held a handkerchief to dry the widow's tears. Sadly, the murder went unsolved, and Mr. King had the dubious distinction of being the first resident buried in the new Bonanza City Cemetery.

During the Victorian era, it was customary for mourning wives to wear black clothing, known as widow's weeds, for an entire year as a sign of respect. But before the ink was dry on Mr. King's death certificate, Elizabeth let her hair down. The new "Lizzy" began wearing colorful dresses that hugged her shapely figure

Agnes Elizabeth King and the Baron of Bonanza
enjoyed tea for two while Mr. King was gone on business.
Author's Collection.

like a second skin. With a mind for business and a body for sin, she opened a billiard saloon. Reinventing herself proved to be her ticket to ride, as the Yankee Fork Gaming Club soon became a popular watering hole. The merry widow then hired British brides to dance with Bonanza's wayward Romeos, and her second business, the new Yankee Fork Dance Hall, was also a sweeping success. For the betterment of Bonanza, she became a philanthropist and generously donated to the poor and needy.

But bringing wine, women, and song into Bonanza City angered pious citizens, who soon took their beef to the mayor. Yet, he only turned a deaf ear. Then came the day when Mayor Franklin surprised Lizzy with an engagement gift. A golden locket, which dangled from a precious string of rare, black pearls. And tucked inside the golden heart was a miniature portrait of Lizzy's angelic face pressed next to the mayor's devilish mug. And then with a sheepish grin, Franklin kneeled on bended knee and proposed to be her fifth husband.

But the weary widow begged for more time. Of course, Franklin agreed to wait, but he worried a younger buck might steal her away. So, he put the squeeze on her by spreading raunchy rumors that she was carrying his love child and that wedding bells would soon be ringing. But this humiliating tactic only drove a painful wedge between them. Then, on the first anniversary of Mr. King's mysterious murder, Lizzy surprised everyone by running away.

Six days later, the sheriff went calling on residents of Bonanza City, deliberating saving the mayor's mansion for last. Upon opening his door, Franklin noticed that the lawman had been crying. The sheriff wiped his eyes and mumbled that he hated to be the bearer of bad news, but that Lizzy had died in bed along with her new husband, a handsome, young bartender whom she'd just hired. A single bullet had pierced both hearts . . . two lovebirds with one stone, so to speak.

Missing from their bridal chamber was Lizzy's golden locket, and so it was reasoned that the honeymooners were killed during a botched robbery. Lizzy's fifth husband was sent to his home state for burial, while she was interred in the Bonanza City Cemetery, next to Mr. King. Again, Mr. Franklin paid for both burials.

But only the preacher and a musician were invited to attend Lizzy's freakish funeral. On a cold and rainy day, the belated bride was laid to rest in a black coffin, lined with scarlet satin. The corpse wore a custom-made ebony wedding gown and matching veil. Dozens of blood-red roses graced the funeral parlor as the organist played spirited tunes. Oddly, Lizzy's new married name was omitted from her tombstone, and the date of her death was noted as that of her ill-fated wedding.

Come to find out, Franklin ordered Lizzy's simple headboard to be engraved this way, so as to mark her new beginning as her fatal ending. As a final insult, the Baron of Bonanza opened a new city cemetery and closed the old one, which held only the graves of Mr. and Mrs. King. And then he renamed the old cemetery Boot Hill. Now, for those of you in the dark, only outlaws and litter bugs were buried in unconsecrated cemeteries known as Boot Hill. These vile boneyards were reserved for bad boys who died in gun battle with their boots on. Boot Hill was never intended for those who'd died in bed while making love. Franklin had deliberately disgraced the memory of Mr. and Mrs. King, and it was the last straw. The devilish mayor was tarred and feathered before being run out of Bonanza City by pitchfork!

Along the Salmon River, Franklin built a simple shack where he panned for gold and pined for long-lost love and fortune. One lonely night, cruel winds began to howl, and, while peering through a frosty window, he thought he heard Lizzy's sweet voice calling his name. But it was only the wicked winds taunting him, once again. Plunking down on a frameless mattress, the drunkard swigged his last drop of whiskey. Lizzy's broken locket, he'd cupped in his sweaty palm. As he gazed at her angelic face, he knew true passion for her. Painfully, he recalled the last time he saw her and how she'd thrown the necklace at him and screamed, "For as long as I live, I never want to see you again! May you and bloody Bonanza burn in bloody hell!" And with that accursed memory, a fateful trigger was pulled . . .

Weeks later on a cold, wintery morning, the concerned mayor of Bonanza, Buck Johnson, made the distant trip to Franklin's cabin with supplies, because the old hermit hadn't been seen around for a spell. Upon opening the cold cabin door, Buck found the old man lying dead in bed. Cupped in Franklin's hand was a golden heart-shaped locket, and in his frozen eyes simmered the haunting reflection of an unforgettable woman.

News of Franklin's welcomed suicide spread to Bonanza City like wildfire. So, the Boot Hill Cemetery was reopened so that the former home-wrecking mayor could be suitably buried between Mr. and Mrs. King. But this was a big mistake! Because not long after Franklin's burial, horrible screeching and wailing resounded from the Boot Hill Cemetery. Apparently, a bullet hole and a coffin lid couldn't keep a good woman down, because Lizzy got the last laugh by reinventing herself, once again. Not only was her restless spirit heard laughing, crying, and screaming, but she was also seen wearing a black wedding dress and matching veil! It was Lizzy all right. And she had an axe to grind. They say that "hell hath no fury like a woman scorned," and so it was with Lizzy's restless spirit! Night after night, the banshee's incessant wailing drifted into the village, and townsfolk dearly suffered without rest. Windows were shuttered, and ears were packed with balls of cotton. But these desperate measures did little good, and so, most folks packed their bags and relocated to the neighboring mining hub of Custer.

Then, on the anniversary of Lizzy's unsolved murder, a sudden wildfire blazed through Bonanza! Two years later, a second inferno torched the town. After being twice baptized by fire, only a spattering of buildings remained. True to Lizzy's ominous words, Bonanza suffered from this accursed hell!

Finally, a lookout tower was built, which still stands guard above the historic ghost towns of Bonanza City and Custer. Today, this fire lookout tower is one of only a few remaining in the Rockies. But it stays open for good reason. It serves to protect tourists from the banshee's fiery spirit! Apparently Lizzy won't rest in peace until she's healed her broken heart of gold. And so it goes.

FOUNTAIN OF SECRETS

The boundaries which divide life and death are at best, watery and vague. Who shall say where one ends and the other begins.

—Edgar Allan Poe

Spread the news! A dead man made contact with the living . . . a century after his death! This ghost story began along the gurgling banks of Fountain Creek, where a fine carpenter by the name of Jack Spicer built the finest mansion anyone in Fountain Valley had ever seen. Spicer lived in the caretaker's cabin behind the stately Loomis manor. One fateful day, he was working in the garden when he met the woman of his dreams: a rich man's daughter. Hovena "Luna" Loch was as lovely as her lyrical name. She'd come by the Loomis estate to pick apples, and when she smiled, the handsome carpenter fell head over heels in love.

Days passed, but Jack couldn't stop thinking about the bewitching beauty. After asking around the town of Fountain, he soon learned that Luna hadn't spoken for years. As a child, she'd been struck dumb after her ranch was attacked by revengeful Utes. Ever since that awful tragedy, she'd only speak through the haunting piano music she played.

Jack was a wizard on the fiddle. And so the duo began making beautiful music together at church functions. One fateful evening, Luna had a horseback-riding date, but her fiancé failed to meet her at the church as planned. With a heavy heart, she hung her head low and sat crying upon the chapel steps . . . until she felt prying eyes burning a hole in the back of her head. Glancing over her shoulder, she spied a shadowed figure silhouetted in the stone archway. She was frightened but came to recognize that the bystander was handsome Jack.

Lovingly, he wrapped his strapping arms around her and cooed: "There, there, sweet angel . . . I never want to see my musical muse unhappy." After pulling a red bandanna from a back pocket, he wiped away salty tears. But the soiled cloth stained her cheek red. Chuckling, Jack teased, "OOPS! I accidently

A dark secret harbored within the
Hovena House haunted the mansion for many years.
Author's Collection.

rouged your cheeks red with blood! Sorry, my dear. Don't worry, I'm not hurt or anything. There must have been a little bear juice left on my hanky. I just bagged a grizzly in Cheyenne Canyon. Shot him right between the eyes! I'll make top dollar off his hide. By gum he was a big boy! Ugly too, and that's why I named him 'Gone John' after your absentee beau. I'm sure this isn't the first time he's stood you up, and it won't be the last."

Jack took off his cowboy hat and gazed at the rising moon. Never in his life had there ever been a more perfect moment. So, on bended knee, the lifelong lothario held Luna's hands in his and then sputtered, "Oh fickle fortune, like the moon you are changeable, ever waxing and waning; hateful life first oppresses and then soothes as fancy takes it; poverty and power melts them like ice. Luna, I've been poor all my thirty-five years. But fate tossed the dice of destiny and fortune now smiles . . . I've suddenly inherited a great fortune! I know you are promised to marry that uncivilized clod, John Sebastian. But you have nothing in common with your kissing cousin, other than blood. John is not sophisticated like you and me. He knows nothing about music, literature, poetry, or love. Now, I realize I wasn't born with a silver spoon in my mouth, like you. But I'm self-educated, cultured, and—let's be honest—I'm much better looking than that lop-eared, cross-eyed drugstore cowboy who stood you up. If you were my gal, things would be different! . . . Will you be my bride?"

But Luna turned a blood-stained cheek away from his pleading eyes and shook her head in blunt refusal. Taking a pencil from her handbag, she scribbled a note saying that she could never bring shame upon the Loch name by marrying outside their bloodline. But Jack was determined to win her heart. So, by the light of a pregnant moon he pleaded to unholy gods. And on that fateful night, Jack made a devilish deal witnessed only by a wide-eyed owl.

A few months later, chapel bells clanged happy song as sweet perfume of apple blossoms wafted through the air. It was Luna's glad wedding day. Standing at the altar awaited a weeping bride and dozens of angry witnesses. John Sebastian was a no-show. And again, Jack was there to dry Luna's tears. Only this time, he did so with a clean handkerchief.

The following morning, Jack purchased the Loomis mansion, renaming the estate "the Hovena House." Flattery won Luna's heart, and the belated bride soon married Jack Spicer in the blooming apple orchard. The happy groom celebrated with a wedding toast, but what took the cake is that he never stopped . . . Which is to say that booze soon became the spice of life for Spicer. Occasionally, he'd sober up long enough for a carpentry job, and he was once paid to guide Vice President Teddy Roosevelt's bear-hunting party. But Jack only heard "PARTY" and drank the entire week they were gone.

Over the years, Jack's habit for drink went to denial. Red faced from shame, Luna suffered alone in silence. At their twenty-fifth wedding anniversary party, Jack made a celebratory toast and then tossed a silver punch bowl over the preacher's head. Adding insult to injury, he ran buck naked through the blooming apple orchard with six guns a blazing. Startled guests scattered like rats from a sinking ship. Thankfully, Luna and their six children found sanctuary at the nearby Loch Ranch.

Later in the evening, Jack rested his pounding head upon his wife's cold pillow. A full moon laughed from a dizzying sky, as a wise owl hooted from the lofty branch of an apple tree. Frightened, Jack knew the devil was coming for his soul, and he sighed aloud:

Fortune and fate—monstrous and empty you whirling wheel, you are malevolent, well-being is vain and always fades to nothing, shadowed and veiled you plague me too, and through the game I bring bare my back to your villainy.

And then, on a wooden piece of decorative crown molding, Spicer spilled his guts, by pencil. The next morning, the drunkard didn't remember a thing as he stared into the angry eye of a shotgun. Luna was standing above with a red face and dark eyes enraged with fire. Suddenly she heaved a deep breath and shattered many years of silence by sputtering "MUR . . . MUR . . . MURDER!"

Like a jackrabbit, Spicer bolted down the dirt road and Luna followed him between crosshairs, until she saw him no more. Finally free, Luna was no longer tongue tied. And it was the last time she ever saw her deadbeat husband!

Years passed while Luna continued living in the mansion. Then on the night of her fiftieth wedding anniversary, the old woman stood admiring a pregnant moon through her bedroom window. The apple orchard was in full bloom and a sweet fragrance flooded her bed chamber. With tears slipping down weathered cheeks, she took a trip down memory lane and recalled all the many years of hardship that Jack had put her through. Painfully, she remembered a long-kept secret, and her frail heart pounded with rage.

After sinking into a rocking chair, Luna gasped her last breath. She was finally at peace. Or was she? Incessant paranormal activity caused the old mansion to sit vacant for many years. Until the fall of 1986, when the dilapidated estate was targeted for the wrecking ball. But fate interceded when a young carpenter and his wife bought the eyesore for a song and a prayer. Yet, their happiness was short lived, after discovering the mansion was terribly haunted. Unrelenting nightmares first bothered the mother, and then the father, followed by three fearful children.

The family began sleeping together in the master bedroom. But every night, haunting piano music would stir them from slumber. And lacy curtains would blow from closed windows, while the incessant thump of a beating heart pounded from within walls. And as if these intrusions weren't frightening enough, a haunting voice began calling for family members—one by one, by name!

Out of mad desperation, the mansion was baptized with holy water and smudged with sacred sage. Shortly thereafter a pipe broke, and raw sewage flooded floors and dripped down walls. Making matters worse, a black deadly mold soon invaded the home. Much of the wooden trim and baseboards had to be replaced. While the carpenter was gutting the master bedroom, his oldest son spied a piece of crown molding that had been torn from the wall and was lying in a scrap pile. Oddly, it seemed to glow in the incoming moonlight, and then the boy noticed that there was a secret message scrawled on the underside of the board that said:

To whoever should happen to find this confession, I John "Jack" Spicer of the city of Fountain in the state of Colorado bring about this shuffle of mortal coil to make this my full confession in hope that when I am gone it may be found and at last clear up the darkest murder that ever embraced one in human murder. On or about the 13th day of March 1893, some four miles north of this city, and two miles east of the foot of Cheyenne Mountain, I did willfully murder with a club one John J. Sebastian for his money and his jewelry worth $5,000 and did drag the mutilated body to a deep ravine some 500 yards distance from the point already mentioned in my confession. My last moments are in prayer for the partial salvation of my soul.

The *Colorado Springs Gazette Telegraph* followed up with updates as the mystery slowly unraveled. Over the following six months, homicide detectives worked hand in hand with local historians to unravel the spellbinding mystery. Cold-case detectives located Spicer's youngest daughter, who was living in nearby Pueblo, Colorado, in a nursing home. At first, the aggravated grandmother was hostile. But finally, she admitted that many had feared her father as a cold-blooded killer. Shortly after the interrogation, the only living child of handsome Jack Spicer and lovely Luna died in her rocker, lifted of a secret burden.

For seven years, the piece of crown molding inscribed with the secret murder confession was held in the district attorney's cold-case files. Finally, owners of the Hovena House petitioned the state and had the evidence returned to them. The murder confession is now displayed under glass at the Fountain Valley Museum, and thankfully the Hovena House is no longer haunted. Apparently, Hovena Luna Loch and Jack Spicer have spilled their fountain of secrets and are finally resting in peace.

SHADES OF
SOUTH PASS CITY

Over the Mountains of the Moon, Down the Valley of Shadow,
"Ride, boldly ride," the shade replied, "If you seek for Eldorado."

—Edgar Allan Poe

At the meeting of crossroads is where the devil always comes calling with trickery. So it's no wonder why a town built upon an intersection of passages became a terribly wicked place.

One of its earliest residents was the Bartlett family. Mr. Bartlett was a widowed minister who traveled from mining camp to mining camp preaching the good word, along with his teenaged daughter, Polly. At Willow Creek, where the immigrant trail crossed Burnt Ranch Road, is where they'd made camp during the summer of 1866.

Daddy and daughter panned for gold, without much luck, until a lone miner came along. He'd made his fortune prospecting in the Medicine Bow Mountains and was on his way home for Christmas. Polly dreamed of being his wife and carrying his checkbook. And she knew the way to a man's heart was through his stomach. So, she fried her intended husband a tempting buffalo burger. After swallowing the first bite, the young lad foamed at the mouth and heaved his last breath.

Nobody had ever croaked from Polly's cooking until that fateful day. After pondering the senseless tragedy, the aspiring chef realized that she'd accidently breaded the burger with rat poison instead of flour! She worried that her pious father would be angry. But Mr. Bartlett was happier than a pig in mud and shouted, "*HALLELUJAH!*"

Daddy Bartlett kissed his doting daughter on the forehead, saying that accidents sometimes happen, but he made her promise to read a cookbook. A passing prayer was whispered over the dead man, and then his clothes were buried

Pretty Polly accidently murdered
twenty-two lovers for pin money and to buy hats!
Author's Collection.

by the river. After shaving the corpse it was butchered and boiled. And then this putrid slop was fed to their hungry hounds. That night, while sitting around a toasty campfire, the old man realized how easy it was making money in the hospitality industry. And with their sudden windfall, he proposed opening a boardinghouse in the nearby mining hub of South Pass City, which was at the crossroads for wagon trains headed to Oregon, California, and Utah.

Timothy Flaherty was the first wayward pilgrim to take advantage of the new Bartlett Boarding House. But after checking in, he soon checked out—Polly had served him a piece of cherry pie, and after just one bite, he'd barfed a bucket of blood. So, she'd rushed to the sink for a wet cloth and cold drink. But by the time she'd returned, Mr. Flaherty no longer needed water . . . or air.

Suddenly, it dawned on the dimwit that instead of making the dough with powdered sugar, she'd used powdered lye. A few hours later, Papa Bear went looking for a midnight snack and found a dead man stuffed in Polly's pantry! Mr. Bartlett called his daughter on the carpet. But when he looked into her big, baby blues, his heart melted like butter. Daddy Bartlett said a passing prayer and butchered the poor fellow. Flaherty's flesh was boiled from bones, and then this Irish stew was fed to their hungry herd. With the windfall found in the dead man's wallet, Mr. Bartlett bought a new bonnet for his daughter's silly head and then added more rooms to Murder Manor.

When Princess Polly went Christmas shopping, she ran into a wealthy Chinese merchant. He was far from home and hurting for company. The next thing you know, he found himself in hot water—boiling hot water—and then Chinese soup was fed to the Bartletts' growing herd of heifers. During the next two years, Polly "accidentally" murdered twenty-two suitors, and her accommodating father dug just as many holes. The Bartletts' dogs enjoyed an unlimited supply of bones to chew on, and their cattle grew as plump as their wallets.

Times were good for the Bartletts, who were living high on the hog. Preacher Bartlett became mayor and was looked upon as a pillar of the community. Meanwhile, Polly was considered the Belle of South Pass City. Her wardrobe closet gushed with elegant gowns, and she had more hats than anyone could ever possibly wear.

Yet, fortune is fickle, and so it was when Barney Fortunes checked into Murder Manor, and then ruined everything when he suddenly disappeared. His parents hired the prestigious Pinkerton Detective Agency to unravel the mystery. But when these special agents came knocking at the Bartletts' boardinghouse, nobody answered. So, they hacked the door open and found an arsenal of poison in Polly's pantry. Even more disturbing was the tangled pile of human bones excavated from the cow pasture. Sadly, an engraved wedding ring identified the bony finger of Barney Fortunes.

The sheriff posted a huge reward for the fugitives, and posters declared that the daddy-daughter gang was wanted: *Dead or Alive*. Seven days later, a retired lawman by the name of Sam Ford tracked the preacher and his daughter to the Hogback River valley. After nightfall, Ford crawled on his belly to get a closer look at the fugitive's camp. Around a roaring campfire, Mr. Bartlett was reading aloud from the book of Exodus, while his wide-eyed daughter sat at his knees and hung on every word. Ford cocked his pistol, and in a heartbeat he shattered the sixth commandment. The preacher shouted "AMEN!" before falling face first into the sizzling pit! Ironically, Bartlett was baptized by fire before being sent to hell.

Polly maintained her innocence throughout Ford's angry interrogation. When questioned about blood stains and poison found in her pantry, the girl meekly insisted that she used arsenic only for exterminating rodents and that the dried blood puddle resulted from a terrible paper cut. Disgusted, the lawman arrested the femme fatale on mere principle. They rode to the closest jail, which had just been built in nearby Atlantic City. Mr. Ford reasoned that at least in a neighboring town, the teenager might get a fair trial.

A week later, on October 7, 1868, a masked stranger in black rode into Atlantic City with murder in mind. As the sun set over the Wind River Mountains, the avenger slipped a sawed-off shotgun through a barred window. The preacher's daughter screamed for mercy, but the Grim Reaper was unforgiving. The man in black escaped like a thief in the night. At least taxpayers were relieved that there wouldn't be a trial. Father and daughter were taken back to South Pass City, where they were buried toe to toe in an unmarked grave.

Townsfolk hoped that the whole matter would soon be forgotten. But the media circus soon began. From coast to coast, boisterous newspaper boys on every street corner shouted:

EXTRA, EXTRA, READ ALL ABOUT IT!

PRETTY POLLY, THE DEVIL'S DAUGHTER . . .

KILLS 22 LOVERS in MURDER MANOR!

Around this time, dozens of shadowy figures began appearing in the South Pass City Cemetery. Since most folks believed that unmarked graves wouldn't be recognized on Judgment Day, the hauntings made perfect sense. Over the years, the spooky rumors persisted and curiosity seekers came from all over the country just to get a glimpse of mysterious "Shadow People." By 1900, the town's infamous phantoms had far outnumbered the living, and South Pass City became a true ghost town in every sense of the word. But South Pass City would never be forgotten, since it was also famed for being home to yet another female hellraiser: Esther Hobart Morris, mother of the women's suffrage movement.

Today, the old ghost town built upon the devil's crossroads is known as South Pass City State Historic Site. Is South Pass haunted? Why wouldn't it be? Witnesses report shadowy figures seen in their peripheral vision. They've also captured compelling photographs of glowing orbs and streaks of light. One of these lost souls must be devilish Polly Bartlett, because she's known to steal kisses, hats, and pocket change. It appears that even while lying in the arms of death, Polly still can't get satisfaction.

HAUNTED HEYBURN PARK

Look before you leap.

—Proverb first recorded in John Heywood's
*A Dialogue Conteinyng the Number in Effect of All the
Prouerbes in the Englishe Tongue,* 1546

The answer is yes. There really is an ancient Indian burial cliff where songbirds deliver sparkling gems to resident ghosts! Although the idea of gift-giving crows may be hard to swallow, this mystery began long ago. On the shores of a shimmering lake in the Bitterroot Mountains, a precious daughter was born to a great chief of the Coeur d'Alene tribe. Named "Chatcolet" after a French missionary, the Indian princess was promised to be married to a mighty chieftain from the neighboring Nez Perce Indian clan. This vital bond would serve as a peace treaty and unite these formerly warring tribes.

Years later, the teenaged princess was exploring the hills surrounding her village when, curiously, she spied a white man for the first time. From a distance she studied the furry-faced trappers until she trusted that a friendship could be forged between them. The big chief enjoyed such novel peace offerings as sweet sugar and strong coffee, and it wasn't long before the tribesmen accepted their new neighbors as white brothers. Princess Chatcolet became especially fond of a handsome young man named Baptist Trudeau. Over the following months, Chatcolet's father knew his daughter's heart had been pierced by the sting of Cupid's arrow. But when she finally confessed her growing feelings for Trudeau, her father banished the deceitful trappers from their village and threatened death if they ever returned. The princess was torn between love and honor.

Despite growing turmoil, Trudeau and Chatcolet agreed to meet clandestinely, as young lovers the world over have always done. Their secret trysting place became a romantic cliff overlooking the lake. The secluded spot had an expansive view that stretched from the emerald green Saint Joe River valley all the way to the snow-covered peaks of the Bitterroot Mountains. This forested overlook was also a sacred Indian burial ground. Molded into the rocky cliffs were deep crevices that harbored ancient Indian graves. These hallowed tombs were decorated with mystical totems crafted from sun-bleached animal bones and colorful bird feathers. Although it was sacred ground, this remote location was an ideal hideaway for their romantic rendezvous because it was rarely visited, except for the occasional burial. The star-crossed lovers enjoyed picnics on the rocks and fed the birds whenever they visited. Sometimes they'd steal away during moonlit evenings and lie in each other's arms while gazing into a canopy of twinkling stars.

Then, on the eve of the maiden's promised wedding to the old chieftain, Chatcolet and Trudeau stole away by light of the moon. Upon reaching the Indian burial cliffs, a holy shaman joined them in secret marriage. They promised to love each other for as long as the wind blew and the grass grew.

News of the secret union was soon discovered, and once smoke signals reached the Nez Perce encampment, the old chieftain was outraged by Chatcolet's cruel rejection. So, he gathered his tribe's fiercest warriors and eagerly rode toward revenge. With hatred pounding in dark hearts, the assassins snuck into the lovers' camp while they were peacefully sleeping in each other's arms. Sadly, Princess Chatcolet was forced to watch as her husband was stripped naked and tortured without mercy. After toying with Trudeau like a spider with a trapped fly, the old chieftain finally pulled his tomahawk and bashed the trapper's head, until brains oozed from his ears. To make it look like an accidental fall, Trudeau's battered body was thrown over the crags.

Hooting and screeching in delight, the victorious scoundrels danced in circles while beating on heaving chests. Sweat dripped from the chieftain's blood-splattered face as he arrogantly bragged of the easy kill. Triumphantly he sneered that the maiden was still to be his bride, and then he sealed his cruel promise with a forced kiss.

But Princess Chatcolet pushed him away with unwilling lips and a cold heart. She knew that she would never allow herself to be touched by the same brutal hands who'd just murdered her beloved husband. Overcome with grief and reluctant to return home in shame, the princess crumpled to the ground in great sorrow. Growing impatient, the old chieftain bellowed for the girl to mount his readied stallion. But the forlorn princess only responded with a blank stare.

Finally, the hoot of an owl shattered the dreadful silence. As if entranced, Chatcolet pulled herself up from the ground and leapt from the perilous cliffs! Horrifying death cries echoed throughout twinkling heavens. The old chieftain howled in great misery and fell to his knees in terrible anguish. Out of respect for Princess Chatcolet, the warriors endeavored to retrieve her broken body for proper burial. They searched the jagged rocks below, but mysteriously her body wasn't found. After three days, they finally gave up the futile hunt.

But as a final insult, they spit on Trudeau's rotting corpse and then rode back to their village with his yellow scalp dangling from an angry spear. Once Chatcolet's father learned of the trapper's cold-blooded murder, he proposed a celebratory feast. But his happiness was soon dashed upon hearing about Chatcolet's tragic leap of faith. Indeed, the chieftain's grief was terrible to behold. He cried in agony, tore at his clothes, and slashed his flesh, but nothing eased his unrelenting suffering. Dark clouds hovered over the lake, fish stopped biting, and animals refused to drink from blood-tainted waters. Finally, Chatcolet's father ordered that his people leave the haunted shores forevermore.

In 1919, US Supreme Court Justice William M. Morgan built a cottage upon the shores of what became known as Chatcolet Lake. Not long after, he began hearing strange sounds that woke him at night. At first he assumed that the mournful cries were a trick of the wind. Then one day the judge learned the legend of Chatcolet Lake from an old Nez Perce Indian friend. Despite the possibility of being laughed off the bench, Morgan put his honorable name on the line and had the spooky legend published in the *Idaho Statesman* newspaper.

Not much has changed at the sacred burial cliffs where the star-crossed lovers perished. The wind still blows, and green grass grows under skies of blue. And you'll still find mysterious offerings of twinkling trinkets, sparkling beads, shiny buttons, and pebbles of glistening glass, scattered upon the rocks. These curious treasures were left there by passing birds as token gifts to the ill-fated lovers. Over time, this mysterious shrine has become a lingering testament to the undying love of Chatcolet and Trudeau. Old-timers claim that while gazing over the lovely valley, those properly attuned with the higher laws of nature can still hear the terrible death cries, which became known as their sorrowful swan song. They say that the timeless lovers still ride on whispering winds and that their kindred spirits will dance above the sparkling waters of Chatcolet Lake forevermore.

TIME-TUMBLING OVER THE OVERLAND TRAIL

What beck'ning ghost, along the moonlight shade
Invites my step, and points to yonder glade?

—Alexander Pope

Legend tells that the Overland Flyer train route was once known to time travelers! The first quantum leaper to tell his story was a noted physician by the name of Doctor King. A learned intellectual, Doctor King often met with other great minds at the gentleman's VIP room of the Union Pacific Railroad Depot, in Cheyenne, Wyoming. One stormy night in 1888, Doctor King was holding court while enjoying cold beer and shucked oysters, when he chuckled, saying: "Believe you me, railroad men are a superstitious lot. Over the years, I've heard my fair share of wild yarns. One of my favorites is a ghost story about Marshall Pass, in Colorado. Once a train neared the summit, the caboose would be charged from behind by a phantom locomotive!

"But the strangest tales were about the Overland line. It's had a dubious reputation since its early beginnings as a wagon road. The Overland route ran along the old outlaw trail, and robberies were common. Steep inclines and sharp twists and turns made the trail extremely dangerous. Deadly accidents and Indian attacks were common. Victims were buried where they'd died, and dozens of hasty graves dotted the roadsides. Once tracks were laid, a tuff engine named Big Boy 4012 took to the rails. That grand engine hauled more than a hundred cars from Omaha to San Francisco in only fifty-six hours. I was only twenty-two years old the first time I rode the Overland Flyer route. I'd been warned of its mysterious reputation but was in a big rush to get to the city by the bay. Just as soon as I entered the club car, this double-chinned spinster yapped her jaws about the route being haunted by a so-called death stalker. I wasn't in the mood for tales of the 'terror train,' and so I moved into an empty car. While drinking a cup of

Big Boy 4012 may have been a time machine!
Author's collection.

tea, I gazed out the open window and saw nothing but the great unknown. Around midnight I was getting drowsy and slipped into the land of nod. I awoke an hour later, shivering and drenched in sweat. I looked up to see a young man sitting at a table, in the same spot where I'd been sitting before my nap. He appeared hazy at first glance, and so I did a double take. That's when I realized that he had an ethereal light around his person, and he was likely a ghost! Stranger still, he seemed familiar. After studying his face, I recognized him. No, he wasn't a deceased relative or a dead friend. The luminescent intruder was my exact self! Slightly older, maybe. But there was no doubt that he was I and I was he. Seeing my ethereal body was altogether perplexing and surreal. But before I could take further study of my astral figure, he'd instantly faded away!"

Doctor King glanced around the table, and with an uneasy smile he mumbled, "Although my hallucination was blamed on fever, I knew that my profound experience was real! But I kept this strange story to myself, until this stormy night, since I feared others might judge me as being insane."

Doctor King blew a ring of smoke, which rested over his shiny, bald head like a hazy halo. After a terribly long pause, he continued his yarn by grumbling, "A few years later, I again saw my ethereal self while riding the Overland Flyer route. During that time, I was working as a traveling physician for the Union Pacific Railroad, out of Green River, Wyoming. One night we were headed on a round trip to Huntington Oregon, which was a 400-mile run. I had just finished signing carbon copies to be sent to the next traveling physician. So I sat on a wooden crate to enjoy a smoke, as pounding rain poured in blinding sheets. The train whistled as it rounded a flooded curve near Pocatello, Idaho. But instead of continuing on the main track, it shot off on the eastbound track and hit the Utah Northern train. The warning whistle screamed. With a prayer on my lips, I slid from my seat. Tumbling passengers, luggage, and boxes flew through the air . . . I was hit in the head.

"The next morning, emergency workers dug my broken body from the wreckage. When I awoke I was lying in a suite at the Plains Hotel, across the street from the train depot, here in Cheyenne. My squire came to see me while I was recuperating. He said that the engineer and firemen on the Utah Northern train were killed, but the crew from our line survived by jumping before impact. Thankfully, none of the passengers were killed, which was amazing since the car I was riding in was crushed like a tin of sardines. The brush with death convinced me to retire from the rails and get a normal desk job. But my squire talked me out of doing such a foolish thing, saying all I really needed was a relaxing vacation. So, I took his advice and the night train, bound for nowhere. As I glanced around the crowded coach, I noticed everyone had their noses stuck in the daily newspaper. On the left side of the cabin, I found a seat near an open window. Across the aisle sat two young men huddled together in whispered conversation. I took notice because they were gossiping about a recent railroad accident on the Overland route. When suddenly, I realized the exciting saga was being told in my exact words! They say that a man won't recognize his recorded voice on a phonograph, but I heard my own and knew it wasn't a convoluted trick of my imagination. I was frightened. But I summoned courage, took a deep breath, and raised my head. Sitting opposite from me was my exact self, in a seated position, and he was wearing the same attire. At first I hoped it was an optical illusion caused by reflective light bouncing off the glass. Sadly, it wasn't so. I wondered if I was losing my mind! Was I dead? Could I be a disembodied spirit? Suddenly, I realized that if I looked into a mirror, I might recognize my own face. So, I stood up and wobbled toward the lavatory, when I felt a bolt of pain shoot through my head. So, I squeezed my eyes shut and shuffled back to my warm seat. A few moments later, I turned to look across the aisle and my body double was gone! The man who'd been sitting next to him had scooted toward the open window. So, I asked what had happened to his companion. After glaring at me like I was nuts, he sneered that he was traveling alone and that I should mind my own business! He asked me to leave and then buried a red face in his newspaper. I was thunderstruck and couldn't explain the uncanny illusion. But I was too tired to pursue the matter. So, I slumped into my seat and pondered the mystery. Drops of cold perspiration beaded on my forehead, and I wanted nothing more than a stiff drink. So, I dashed into the club car for a drop of liquid courage. One shot was followed by another, and another. Again, I heard my own laugh, and goose bumps rippled down my spine! Eerily, I looked across the smoky car and saw myself standing next to an open window! My body double turned to me with questioning eyes, and my hair stood on end. And then, of all things, my doppelganger looked at me like I was the one who was insane! I grabbed a crystal water decanter and threw it at his smirking gaze! The alarming crash sent splinters of glass through the air. He laughed at me with contempt as I sank to the floor in disgust. In angered haste, I'd broken a hanging cabin mirror! After a custodian swept away silvery shards, he alerted another traveling physician, who came to my aid. Doctor Pierce had been riding in the next car and was worried about my state of health and mental condition. With cold fingers, he stuck a glass thermometer into my mouth, and the thin, red line of mercury shot to a hundred and four. After shining a light in my eyes, he asked for my name. But with my delusional fever, I replied only 'I am who I am.'" Doctor King took a swig of whiskey and snorted, "Come to find out, I wasn't crazy after all, because other witnesses on the train also saw my doppelganger. Only they assumed I was traveling with my twin! Apparently, the engineer also had a paranormal twin brother, because he wrote about seeing his body double in the Overland's daily log, hours before he was killed in the derailment!" King opened his leather satchel and extracted an old newspaper article, saying, "It's right here in yellowed, black and white, fellas!"

Headlines for the *Duluth News-Tribune* screamed:

HAUNTED BY HIS OWN GHOST
WEIRD EXPERIENCE OF A RAILROAD MAN
WHO HAS BEEN IN A WRECK

Doctor King passed the newspaper article around his circle of knightly friends, along with a well-worn book—the genius of Mark Twain. After lighting another cigar, he heaved a cloud of blue smoke toward a ceiling fan, saying, "Death soon comes to all who see their own ghost. But I've seen mine on two separate occasions, and I'm still alive, aren't I? So, perhaps my tale isn't a ghost story after all. Maybe the Overland Flyer sent me time-tumbling and I'd become another Yankee who'd landed in King Arthur's Court!"

GLOOM OF DEAD MAN'S GULCH

Seeing is believing.

—Unknown

Believe it or not, a black cloud has shrouded the red sands of Dead Man's Gulch for nearly 150 years! This mystery all began when a man without horse stumbled into the Los Pinos Indian Agency. The scruffy stranger began shaking, and his piercing gray eyes suddenly rolled to the back of his head. A quick-thinking soldier helped him into a steady chair while another poured a cup of hot tea. Much to everyone's surprise, the hulky mountain man sipped with the gentle refinement of an aristocrat. After whipping the corners of his black-bearded lips with a checkered napkin, he thanked them with a soft, effeminate voice and said something like, "I was shivering like a lizard looking for a hot rock . . . Please allow me to introduce myself. My name is Packer. I've been misunderstood all my life. I came into this godforsaken world thirty-one years ago under the name of Alfred. But a drunken tattoo artist misspelled my name as Alferd, and so I've gone by that address ever since. Hell, you can call me whatever you like; just don't call me late for supper! You may have noticed that I don't possess a dainty pinky finger on my right hand in order to properly tip this precious teacup. That's because I lost my tenth digit to frostbite during the Civil War. After being discharged, due to my chronic epilepsy and horrible flatulence, I became a prospector . . . Although I haven't struck it rich yet, I still have prospects. Just six weeks ago, I went scouting for gold with five others. But soon after hitting the trail, a blinding blizzard separated me from my wayward pals. Those boys were as shy of brains as a terrapin is of feathers. I hope they made it back to civilization, but I doubt it. Those mountains will eat you alive . . . I'm the kind of man who can track a bear through running water or a bee through a blizzard, but hell's bells, wild game couldn't be found. Thank heaven, I somehow survived on pine resin. My belly shrunk to where it couldn't chamber a liver pill. And it was colder than a witch's tit in a brass bra. Thankfully, I found refuge. In a comfy cave, I hibernated with a grizzly that kept hogging my covers. After forty-five days I made my way back to civilization, and now I'm sitting here with you fine people. But I expect that I'll be hitting the trail again, come morning. If my fellow comrades come along, just tell them I'll be waiting for them in hell!"

Suddenly, a plump horsefly caught Alferd's shifting eyes. With the quick dart of a tongue, the mountain man plucked the offending trespasser from midair and washed it down with a gentle swig of tea. General Adams was impressed with the mountain man's uncompromising survival skills. Yet, he was puzzled why the war veteran had refused a hot meal (other than the measly horsefly). And the mountain man didn't look emaciated, as one would expect. But Adams just shrugged off these astute observations.

The next morning, Packer was gone without the courtesy of saying goodbye. Coincidently, an Indian scout dropped by later that morning carrying a sack of dried human flesh that he'd found hidden nearby. Adams was convinced that something sinister was at play. So, he sent a posse of skilled trackers to investigate. At a scenic overlook Adam's men enjoyed a picnic while gazing upon the beauty of Lake Cristobal. However, the rib-sticking meal didn't stay with them for long, because once they hiked around a river bend, all three men lost their lunch. Much to their horror, strips of human flesh hung drying from surrounding tree branches, and swarms of hungry flies enthusiastically feasted on the dead. Five victims lay side by side, next to an ashen circle of cold stones. Ripped clothing exposed sun-bleached bones and patches of missing flesh. Scattered around the fire pit were pots and pans. The snow-white ground of this cruel kitchen was stained by a pool of frozen blood. A black crow fluttered down and plucked a frozen eyeball from a withered face and then squawked in delight before flying off with the gruesome treasure. The brazen bird wasn't the only thief to have raided the campsite, since none of the victims had wallets. Suddenly, a dark cloud sank over the gulch, as if Mother Nature desired to cloak the despicable crime scene.

Meanwhile, in the nearby settlement of Saguache, Alferd found a saloon and bought multiple rounds from different wallets. On a hunch, the sheriff arrested the scruffy newcomer and threw him in the jailhouse. Once General Adams arrived, Alferd's confession sounded something like, "I only skinned my friends and stole their money, *after* they were dead. Our ill-fated journey began in Provo with a rag-tag team of twenty-one hopeful prospectors. We headed east toward the promising gold fields of Breckenridge. But by the end of January, we'd only arrived at the halfway point. Outside the town of Delta, we stopped by the Ute Indians' camp. Chief Ouray warned that it would be bad medicine to cross over the Rockies in midwinter, and he offered shelter until springtime. But some of us got antsy. So, for a reasonable price, I offered to escort five of the prospectors over the treacherous mountains. But three days into our journey, we became hopelessly lost in the wilderness . . . We tried to fish and hunt, but game was scarcer than a two-dollar bill. A week later, we eyeballed each other like we were

Left: Griffins brother standing at his grave.
Right: Griffins grave.

looking at a menu. As far as I can recollect, old man Swan was the first man to be sacrificed for the nourishment of others. I came back from gathering firewood, lured by the sweet smell of bacon, and found the gang roasting strips of human flesh. They'd selected Mr. Swan because he was the oldest and couldn't put up a fight. A few days later, Mr. Miller furnished our next meal. As the youngest, he was the most palatable. The tender flesh of his nipples was succulent and sweeter than wine. Mr. Humphries came next . . . Mr. Bell attacked him while he slept. After that meal, I slept with one eye open. Then one afternoon I returned to camp and found Mr. Bell grilling a pair of human feet over the flames and realized they'd once belonged to a strapping young buck whom we'd called California. And then there were two . . . Mr. Bell and myself. We agreed not to eat each other . . . but once I heard his stomach growling, I grabbed Swan's old gun and shot my campmate, making me the last man standing. When you eat someone, they become a part of you. It's a sacred communion and the ultimate sacrifice.

Since I didn't want to leave Bell behind, I cut him into strips, packed what I could carry, and made my way back to the Los Pinos Indian Agency."

After his startling confession, Packer agreed to escort General Adams to the camp of doom, come morning. But Adams soon learned that Packer was an escape artist. For nine long years, Packer lived on the lam. Until 1883, when the carefree cannibal was enjoying a spot of tea at Fort Fetterman, and a soldier recognized him by a missing pinky and feminine voice. Days later, the nine-fingered, sissy-voiced cannibal was in Lake City fighting for his life. During the spectacular trial, the cannibal was cool under pressure but acted unremorseful. It's no wonder he was pronounced guilty of premeditated murder and sentenced to dance with the hangman.

Upon his sentencing, the disgusted judge is remembered to have said, "Packer, ye Republican, man-eating son of a bitch, there was just seven Democrats in Hinsdale County and ye ate five of them, damn ye! I sentence you to be hanged by the neck until dead, dead, dead . . . Whether your murderous hand was guided by the misty light of the moon or the flickering blaze of a campfire only you can tell. No eye saw the bloody deed performed. No ear save your own caught the dying cries of your victims . . . to the sickening details of your crime I will not refer. Silence is kindness. I do not say things to harrow your soul for I know you have drunk from the cup of bitterness to its very dregs . . ."

In a twist of fate, Packer was saved from the hangman. But until his natural death from stomach problems, he swore innocence and hungered for a governmental pardon. And that's why he still haunts Dead Man's Gulch! Because legend tells us that even today, a dark cloud still lingers over blood-stained sands of Dead Man's Gulch. Perhaps Alferd still has a bone to pick!

GRIM REAPER OF LOON CREEK

Nothing is so bothersome as a secret.
—French proverb

Loon Creek has a loony secret . . . it's haunted! Long ago, ghosts of Loon Creek began menacing a lonesome laundry man. Fearing insanity, Sing Wah recorded these strange occurrences in his cherished journal. His last entry told of a cold, winter night where he wrote, "In darkness, you're cold but can't feel it. Because when you see, you suffer . . . I'm thankful it's a moonless night."

From the frosty window of his cabin, he gazed at surrounding mountains, blanketed with snow. The rugged road to his log shanty hung from a cliffside, and the abundance of snow made it impassable during the winter. Sing Wah shivered as he recalled happier days. Just one year earlier, in 1878, his family left their ancestral homeland and opened a Chinese laundry in the Yankee Fork region. Since then, he'd known only cold comfort. Turning from the window, he tossed back his long pigtail and shuffled to the fireplace. Although still a young man, Sing Wah felt older than the hills. It was hard to sleep with an empty belly and heavy heart.

Around midnight, he heard a desperate rapping on his cabin door. A customer calling at that late hour was unusual. Sing Wah kept his eyes upon fading coals and prayed that the intruder would soon leave. But the knocking continued until the front door creaked open, and a tall, thin man glided into the room. Wearing a black overcoat, his hooded head cast a shadow over his weathered face. Startled, Sing Wah tried not to show fear. After rising from his rocking chair, the lanky youth straightened his robe and bowed. The stranger nodded silently in return greeting. Sing Wah shivered and commented about the cold night, and the towering newcomer nodded in quiet agreement. Out of goodwill, Sing Wah offered the wayward traveler a cup of hot tea. But the old man only shook his head in blunt refusal as screaming winds rattled glass in the window frame.

Miners at Loon Creek were haunted by the Grim Reaper!
Author's Collection.

The young man feared a supernatural connection and shuddered with a vague sense of apprehension. After a long silence he stammered, "Many strange things have been happening around the mining camps . . . this winter has been harsh and dozens have died. The fever struck and accidents have taken their toll. Just last week, nine Chinese miners died upon the banks of Loon Creek. One victim was found without arms, legs, or a head—his death was not accidental. Bad men dressed as native warriors blame the assault on Sheep Eater Indians. They charged into camp wearing war paint and shouting battle cries before stealing away with flour, rice, beans, and beef. They set buildings on fire. These vandals are still at large, and this worries me. Perhaps Tsez Moi, the god of evil spirits, is to blame."

Sing Wah poked the dying fire with a distant look in his eyes and whispered, "My youngest brother just passed over to the land of flowers. He was the last of my small clan to die under mysterious circumstances. I couldn't dig his grave because of the frozen ground. So, my little brother along with the rest of my family is buried beneath this shanty." Sing Wah pointed to the wooden floor, saying, "That trapdoor opens to a sinkhole where my kinfolk are gathered in process of decay. But I hope one day to have their bones cleaned, lacquered, and sent to China. My kinfolk will rebury them in our homeland. We believe that our bones must rest where we were born. If they do not, then our soul cannot rest in peace.

Sing Wah took a long drag from his clay pipe and released a gray ribbon that danced around his crowning black beanie. "I'm ashamed to admit that before burying my younger brother, I chopped off his pigtail and nailed it to the overhead beam . . . Do you see that dangling braid of black, interwoven with colorful silk? Well, according to our Chinese tradition, severing our pigtail is like cutting the tail from a kite . . . Neither a kite nor the human soul can take flight without a tail. Now, I'm sorry for committing this selfish act. I thought nailing his pigtail to the ceiling beam would tether his spirit to our cabin, where I'd enjoy his company. But keeping my brother's soul as a paranormal prisoner was an unforgiveable sin. My brother's spirit is angry and his menacing has caused much trouble."

Sing Wah glanced over at his silent witness and wondered what he'd been thinking. Wicked winds gained speed and raced down the mountainside. But after airing his dirty laundry, so to speak, Sing Wah somehow felt warmer. He arose from his rocking chair and gazed through the ice-chapped window. A hoot owl warned of the late hour, and goodwill beckoned him to offer the wayward traveler sanctuary. The old man nodded in acceptance, shuffled over to a frameless mattress, and rolled into a cocoon. His long beard wrapped around his black overcoat like a silvery spiderweb.

Sing Wah lit a candle and said his nightly prayers. He begged for merciful relief from worry and then went to bed. The fire grew low, and dying flames projected spectral visions upon the cabin walls. Dancing shadows resembling fearsome timber wolves and mountain lions made his heart race faster than rippling waters of the Salmon River. Like his ancestors, Sing Wah could read omens, and he knew that danger lurked nearby.

An hour later, an alarming screech rattled from beneath the shanty. Like Lazarus rising from the dead, Sing Wah sat upright, rubbed his groggy eyes, and noticed the trapdoor easing open. A strange glowing light and the essence of rotting flesh pervaded the room. He gasped for air just as howling winds swept down the chimney, scattering ashes throughout the chamber. After the dust settled, the phosphorous image of a Chinese boy arose from the trapdoor. Dressed in a radiant silver tunic, the demon child ran around in circles, like a crazed rabbit. Sing Wah cowered under the covers upon recognizing the demon child as the ghost of his younger brother! The imp's glassy eyes rolled upward in their angular slits as they fastened upon the dangling pigtail. In a frenzy, the ghost boy leapt and attempted to grab the illustrious black braid from the lofty beam. After three running leaps, he snagged his prize and howled with triumph! With the pigtail grasped between yellowed fangs, the dirty devil danced around the room like a pagan god celebrating an unholy Mass. His talon-like claws ripped pillows, and bird feathers took flight. Joyfully, he banged on pots and pans before untying his britches and dousing the fire! Stinging clouds of urine vapor caused the old man to cough and stir in his self-made cocoon. A split second latter, a booming gunshot silenced the chaos. Like a prisoner cut from the gallows, the naughty ghost boy fell back into the abyss, and the trapdoor slammed with a thunderous clap!

The following morning, a party of miners on their way to new diggings passed through the camp. However, Sing Wah didn't answer the door. Being worried, they broke a window and crawled inside, only to find their Chinese friend dead in bed. At first they didn't recognize the young laundryman, since he'd aged many moons. They surmised that a bullet came from the opposite side of the room, struck the ceiling beam, and ricocheted downward, striking Sing Wah between the eyes. The latched door was locked from the inside, and there weren't any tracks in fresh snow. Yet, no signs of forced entrance. The only explanation was that the perpetrator slithered down the chimney or tunneled under the house. Although plausible, both theories were unreasonable. Nothing else in the one-room shanty lent explanation for the tragedy, save for an old black overcoat covered with long strands of gray hair. Inside the moldy garment lay the stiffening body of Sing Wah. But how could this be? Unless the overcoat had been worn by death's disguise!

This mystery was never solved. And even to this day, loony secrets still haunt Loon Creek.

GHOULS GULCH

Footfalls echo in the memory, down the passage we did not take,
towards the door we never opened, into the rose garden.

—T. S. Eliot

History has a way of repeating itself, and so it seems that Ghouls Gulch becomes haunted time after time. But how did this uncanny mystery all begin?

First known as Brown's Gulch, the mining camp broke ground around 1859. This burgeoning empire was surrounded by gold and silver mines. King of them all was the "Terrible Mining Company," which took great advantage of employees. For example, at the company store, staples such as coffee, flour, and sugar cost twice what they did in nearby Silver Plume or Georgetown. Stuck between a rock and a hard place, disgruntled miners became more like indentured servants than valued workers. Sadly, they could never save enough money to escape from this hellhole. At a time before unions, working conditions were deplorable. Miners weren't trusted or respected. Their pockets and lunch buckets were often searched without permission. And if precious nuggets were found, everyone paid for the thievery with docked wages.

Upon sunrise an annoying bugle call jolted the miners from peaceful slumber. Sleepy-eyed workers trudged a steep toll road that led to the summit of Sherman Mountain. The mouth of the 7:30 mine stood 1,200 feet above Brown's Gulch. Every step was carefully measured—the trail was steep enough to dizzy a mountain goat. Whenever man or beast tumbled over the cliff, a swinging bell clanged. This warned those on the lower path to be on alert for falling rocks and bodies. After the dust cleared, coworkers would remove their hats for a brief moment of respectful silence, and then life would continue for everyone except for the dearly departed. Few men splattered upon the canyon floor, since most landed on protruding ledges. Sometimes it took several days for a victim to die from dehydration or starvation. Meanwhile, they'd linger upon these lofty roosts, like a fly trapped in a spider's web. Blood-curdling cries for sweet merciful death

The lonesome grave of Clifford Griffin stands ten feet tall
and was made famous in *Ripley's Believe It or Not!*
Author's Collection.

could be heard echoing throughout the narrow canyon. But there was never a call for help, since valiant rescue was impossible. Hopeless coworkers had no other choice but to turn their backs and close their ears.

These protruding ledges became like hanging tombstones and served as a constant reminder that death literally hung over everyone's shoulders. The ever-present stench of decay was unnerving. But this was just the harsh reality of life and death in Brown's Gulch.

One fine day, the head honcho for the Terrible Mining Company became a mysterious Englishman by the name of Clifford Griffin. Tall, dark, and handsome, all the single ladies wanted to date the wealthy bachelor. But the misanthrope rarely socialized and always insisted that his heart belonged to another. In the beginning, Griffin was a fairly decent boss. On Christmas Day everyone got a turkey, and on New Year's Eve he picked up the bar tab from Silver Plume to Georgetown.

One day Clifford was hiking up the toll road with a few employees when he stumbled across a disturbing scene. A wild critter had chewed off its own foot to escape from a steel trap. Clifford picked the tiny foot from an angry hinge and mumbled, "Nothing left to do but go mingling with the stains," and then he threw the bloody foot over the cliff. As time passed, he became paranoid and watched over his employees like a hawk. He even built his lofty cabin next to the mouth of the cliffside 7:30 mine, in order to keep a closer watch over his golden empire. His lofty log cabin appeared rustic from the outside, but it was richly furnished with priceless antiques. Imported rugs warmed hard wooden floors, and windows sparkled with precious stained glass. Bookshelves were stuffed with leather-bound classics. Behind the bachelor's homestead was the inspiration of a towering waterfall, and in front was a rock precipice that hung over Brown's Gulch, like an eye in the sky.

And it was upon this lofty stage that Griffin played nightly concerts. Every evening at sundown, the first strain of his quivering bow signaled that the performance was about to begin. Miners would step outside their homes and gather around huddled campfires. With the wave of his top hat, Griffin would greet his reluctant audience, and then the torture would begin. Fiddle strings were molested by a wobbly bow, and this horrific screeching sank over the canyon like a lead balloon. His piercing tunes were so awful that stomachs turned and ears bled. Recklessly the dreary music whined until a canopy of stars filled night skies. Employees resented the melancholy marathons because they got no rest. But to whom could they complain, since the mad musician was their tyrannical boss?

One terrible evening, a fire erupted in Brown's Gulch. Bells clanged as shrieks and screams for help rang throughout the mining camp. A bucket brigade of volunteer firefighters was quickly formed. It was a race against time as skies darkened. And just like the Roman emperor Nero, Griffin played his frantic fiddle while his empire burned. As gray ashes and orange embers swirled into darkened skies, the tyrant danced wickedly above the mining hamlet, like a cat on a hot tin roof. Sparks flew from his fingertips and it looked as though he was channeling the devil himself! The feverish music bounced off the canyon walls, shattering windows and pounding ear drums. The horrendous screeching raged on until his furrowed brow beaded with sweat and bony fingers dripped with blood.

Finally, the towering inferno was arrested. Thankfully, there was minimal damage, and everyone heaved a great sigh of relief. Everyone except for the maniac musician who played his unstoppable fiddle like there was no tomorrow. Weary miners scurried inside cabins and buried heads under blankets and pillows. But no sound barrier could cut the aggravating din. Until around midnight, when this theater of pain was abruptly silenced, and a blanket of peace fell over Brown's Gulch when the sandman finally came knocking.

Come morning, there was no sunrise call by a jubilant bugler. Employees rushed up the hillside, afraid of what they'd find. Just outside Clifford's cabin, they discovered their boss lying face down in a shallow hole. At his side was a blood-splattered violin and an empty bottle of whiskey. Griffin had a hole in his heart. Although his gun was never found, lawmen figured the weapon had bounced off the cliff.

Later that morning, Clifford's besotted brother stepped forward in order to shed light on the mystery, and he said something like, "I know not if Clifford started the barn fire. But I do know that my brother was haunted by inner demons . . . Crossing an ocean did nothing to make him forget the haunting memory of a long, lost love. Last night was the tenth anniversary of his ill-fated wedding. Sadly, his childhood sweetheart left him standing at the altar. Mystified by her cruel rejection, my brother rushed to her hotel room and found his fiancé lying in their bridal bed. Wearing a lacy, white wedding gown, she looked like a sleeping angel . . . But Clifford refused to believe that his belated bride was dead. So, he locked himself in her chamber for three days, until lawmen axed the door open and pried the groom's stubborn arms from around his bride's stiffened corpse. After examining dark shadows around the fallen angel's neck, detectives reasoned she'd been strangled. But a motive was never found, and the book was soon closed on the hopeless investigation. Was it possible that my brother had something to do with his fiancé's brutal murder? I wouldn't think so. But nobody knew Clifford's dark heart. He never spoke of the terrible tragedy but clearly channeled his madness into the sinister music that he played . . . May Clifford Griffin finally rest in peace." A scribbled suicide note requested that he be buried in the crude grave of his own making.

But the touching honor didn't placate Clifford's restless spirit—the very next evening, wicked violin music erupted from the cliffs! Alas, Clifford had returned for an encore. Night after night, the phantom fiddler was seen as a dancing skeleton, wearing a tuxedo and top hat! And his haunting melodies summoned an unholy guard. This army of dead miners arose from the hanging tombstones and joined the phantom fiddler's spirited dance! Dead men shrieked, moaned, and rattled chains in harmony with Griffin's mournful violin.

Living employees of the Terrible Mining Company begged that something be done about the dancing dead. So, a colossal monument was erected in the musician's timeless memory. Standing ten feet tall, Griffin's memorial teeters on the edge of a towering cliff. And from the canyon floor, the tremendous tombstone appears to be hanging in midair! The inscription reads:

CLIFFORD GRIFFIN
Son of Alfred Griffin, ESQ of Brand Hall, Shropshire, England
Born July 2, 1847, Died June 19, 1887
And in Consideration of His Own Request Buried near This Spot.

But the astonishing monument did nothing to placate the phantom fiddler and his skeletal band of ghouls. And so, the terrible hauntings continued.

Today, Brown's Gulch is better known as Ghouls Gulch. Remarkably, the old toll road leaving from the ghost town of Silver Plume and leading to the cliffside mine is more treacherous than ever before. It's now overgrown and covered in loose mining tailings, but the breathtaking view is well worth the hike. That is, if you're not afraid of musical ghouls or of falling on hanging tombstones! And if you plan on paying the phantom fiddler a visit, be sure to bring a few token coins to leave on his massive tombstone. Because legend tells that all those who refuse to pay the toll fee will be pushed from the cliffs! Apparently, greedy Griffin is still looking for recruits to join his spirited band of ghouls.

History has a way of repeating itself. And so it seems that Ghouls Gulch is doomed to remain haunted, time after time . . .

CURSE OF THE
UINTAH MOUNTAINS

Great fortune brings with it great misfortune.
—George Herbert

Ute Indian legend tells that the Uintah Mountains are haunted by a commanding spirit known as "Keeper of the Uintahs." Over the years, this vigilante American Indian ghost has murdered many for destroying the land he protects! This all began long ago, when Spanish conquistadors came storming into the Rockies. These silver-clad warriors dug prospecting holes throughout the Uintah Mountains and soon discovered precious silver and gold. Enslaving native Indians to do their dirty work was all a part of their grand plan. After suffering through many years of tyranny, the natives finally banded together and declared war. And their fearless leader? A great chieftain by the name of Colorow Ignacio Ouray Wakara, meaning the Great Black Hawk. Under his astute command an elite militia was formed. These fearsome warriors sought revenge against their hated enemies by raiding Spanish encampments, missions, and forts. After becoming master over their oppressors, the Great Black Hawk was greatly revered among his people.

Then one fateful night, the chieftain had a prophetic dream about white men wearing tall hats. Not long after, winds of change blew wagon trains upon the shores of Salt Lake. The Church of Latter Day Saints befriended the Utes because they believed native people were the so-called seeds of Abraham. Mormon leader Brigham Young and the Great Black Hawk shared a peace pipe and came to agree on many things, such as their shared hatred for Uncle Sam and the joy of many wives.

Eventually, the Mormon minister convinced his bronzed brother to become a Christian. But being baptized still didn't make the Great Black Hawk give up his wanton ways, such as stealing horses and terrorizing trespassers. Even so, Wakara more than made up for his sins by giving a mountain of gold to the church.

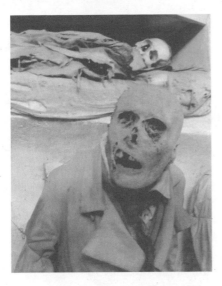

The long-lost Rhoades Gold Mine served as a sacred burial tomb for Ute chieftains. One chamber held the mummified remains of thieving trespassers. *Author's Collection.*

He did this by leading a Mormon rancher by the name of Thomas Rhoades to a sacred site in the Uintah Mountains known as "Carre Shin Ob." These secret burial caves were inside an ancient Spanish prospecting hole.

Chief Wakara and Rhoades wandered through meandering tunnels by flickering torchlight. One cavern held former trespassers, and dozens upon dozens of corpses were found in various stages of decay. Most of the victims had been tortured before death, since their corpses had been dismembered and disemboweled. Still another chamber of chillers held natural stone beds, where the mummies of great chieftains were perfectly preserved in full battle regalia. And then came a chamber filled to the brim with sparkling nuggets of gold. Needless to say, the pious rancher was impressed.

But the Great Black Hawk had no interest in glittering rocks. He only wanted to help the church, or so he said. Perhaps he was hedging his bet on getting into heaven *and* into the happy hunting grounds. Whatever the reason, Wakara bade Rhoades to keep the sacred mine a secret, insisting that only the rancher could know about its hidden location.

Two years later, Chief Wakara died of natural causes, and his mournful funeral became almost as memorable as the mighty chieftain himself. Thousands of natives tore their clothes and slashed flesh as a sign of great respect for their supreme leader. The body of the mighty chieftain lay upon a fragrant bed of pine branches. Shimmering gold paste was painted over the chieftain's face and hands. His golden-hued buckskins were adorned with sparkling gold nuggets and brilliant hawk feathers. A fire crackled in a nearby pit, where ceremonial herbs such as sweet sage, yucca, and kinnikinnick burned in his honor. Thrown onto a bonfire were fifteen of his finest horses, so that the mighty chieftain could ride stylishly into the happy hunting grounds. Two of his favorite wives were sealed inside his tomb . . . even though they weren't dead. His lesser-loved wives didn't complain. Wakara was blessed with many children, but only his three youngest were tucked inside the chamber. Their cries, it was believed, would frighten away evil spirits.

The chieftain's burial mound was on an eastern cliff overlooking the peaceful Mormon community known as Mountain Meadows. Not long after Chief Wakara was buried, a Mormon militia disguised as native Indians slaughtered 120 pioneers. Latter-Day Saints blamed this tyranny on the Utes. After the massacre, bewildered natives regarded Mountain Meadows as bad medicine. So, the loving brothers of Chief Wakara broke into the chieftain's tomb and spirited away with the royal mummy.

The Great Black Hawk was reburied in the sacred mine, and the Utes severed their friendship with Rhoades. Furthermore, the Utes threatened that a deadly curse would befall any white man who trespassed into the Uintah Mountains. But the allure of easy riches was too tempting. Every month during a dark moon, Rhoades secretly rode a packed mule into the Uintahs and returned with buckets of gold. During one ill-fated expedition, the Utes killed the rancher's youngest son. Even so, Rhoades continued with his deceit. Although the rancher became deathly ill, he never made the connection that he'd been jinxed by ancient Hoodoo. Until one day when he discovered a black hawk feather tucked under his bed pillow. Suddenly he remembered how he'd also found a black feather in his son's belongings, just before his murder. And that's when the rancher realized his days were numbered. Just before he passed away, Rhoades told his oldest son where to find the sacred mine, but begged him not to take any more gold from the Utes. But Rhoades's eldest son was also tempted by riches, and he also mined the ancient hole. Until he suddenly died, and secrets of the sacred mine were lost.

Since then, many have searched in vain for the mysterious "Rhoades Mine," including outlaws in the Butch Cassidy Gang. Old-timers claim there's enough treasure left in this ancient mine to pay off the national debt! Yet, this area now lies under strict protection of the Uintah Mountain Indian Reservation. Trespassing on private lands is bad medicine, no matter how tempting the allure of easy riches may be.

Over the years, countless victims have died while searching for the long-lost treasure. Now and then, local newspapers relay spooky stories about greedy tourists going for gold and then disappearing, never to be found. And whenever a trespassing thief is discovered dead, a black feather is always near the corpse. This warning sign came to be known as the "Curse of the Great Black Hawk."

One of the first times this happened was back in 1865, when a dead prospector was found with a tomahawk in his back and a black hawk feather in his mouth. The following summer, still another miner suffered the same fate. And several esteemed authors have also been subjugated, including Gale Rhoades, a descendent of Thomas Rhoades. Gale spent over forty years researching information about his family's namesake mine. In September 1988, Mr. Rhodes was adding final touches to a revealing book, and three weeks before his life's work was to be published, the author suddenly expired. A black feather was discovered tucked inside his manuscripts. And don't forget another aspiring author by the name of George Thompson. Like the others, he'd also spent much of his life searching for the sacred mine. But just before his revealing book was to be published in 1995, he died in a freakish car accident. Eerily, a black feather was found on the backseat of his vehicle. Coincidence? Of course not!

In conclusion, if you ever get a hankering to search for the sacred Rhoades mine, you might want to think again!

RESURRECTION AT ISLETA

You can't keep a good man down.
—Genesis 40–41

You can't keep a good man down, as the old saying goes. And this adage seems to be especially true in the village of Isleta. Long ago, Spanish monks had the foresight to document the miracles of Isleta. One story tells of a funeral held by Chief Dripping Water, who stood before a village of mourners saying something like, "Dear friends, I know many of you have traveled here to the Manzono Mountains from afar. Thank you for attending this memorial service honoring our dear friend, Padre Juan de Padilla. He was a prominent member of our village, and so we are burying him here at the chapel of Isleta. Father Padilla may be gone, but he will never be forgotten. The holy man has left an indelible legacy of love and compassion. It's too bad that we killed him, but we did so because his wisdom frightened us. Conking him on the head with a stack of Bibles was Big Rock's idea. He also used a knife to stab Padre Padilla in the back, while he was kneeling in prayer. I'm sure that our dear Padre Padilla has already forgiven Big Rock since yesterday, as he was a great and good man. Father Padilla taught us not to hit one another, and that knives were for cutting our food and not for stabbing our friends. But apparently Big Rock wasn't listening on that day . . . Padre Padilla helped us build huts and taught us how to farm our fields. Many moons ago, Padre Padilla crossed over great waters with silver-clad conquistadores, led by Coronado. These warriors were bad. They hungered for twinkling rocks of silver and gold. They ate at our table and drank from the blood of our people, and then set out for the land where streets were paved with precious gold and were lined with sparkling gemstones. During the arduous journey, a Peruvian Indian known as the Turk kept getting them lost. I think the Turk was just stalling for time, because the Seven Cities of Cibola and the lost land of Quivira are nothing more than silly fairy tales, told to passing tourists to get them out of our hair. Once Coronado's army reached the land of sunflowers and windstorms, he ordered the Turk's execution. First, the Turk was hit over the head with a stack of Bibles. But when that method didn't work, the misdirected tour guide was stabbed in the back while kneeling in prayer. The Turk is no more. Coronado is no more. Father Padilla is no more. Life is strange. But Father Padilla was a good man. After leaving Coronado's army, he appeared among the people of Gallinas Valley, near Santa Fe. Where he came from, no one knew. But he told them he was a Franciscan monk who sailed over great waters and crossed big lands to help native peoples. He lived on a holy mountain known as Hermit's Peak. He declared that while standing upon the summit that an artist would throw down his brush in despair and a poet would lament for lack of words to describe the awe-inspiring view. Father Padilla used pretty words to paint colorful pictures in our heads. He was a great and good man. Too bad we killed him. Anyway, the Gallinas people agreed to help the holy man of brown cloth, and soon the monk had many followers. From a phantom forest of deadwood, they carved a sea of Christian crosses, which lead to the awe-inspiring summit. The holy man became known to the people of Gallinas as Juan de los Cruces, or John of the Crosses. Padre Juan told his followers he'd stay for three years and forty days. But before leaving, he laid out stakes on a path going up to the peak and told his followers that every May 3rd, they were to have a great festival where they should stop at different places along the trail and pray, calling these designated prayer spots 'stations of the cross.' There was a holy spring on the trail where pilgrims could drink blessed waters and pray in peace. Then one day, Padre Padilla left just as suddenly as he'd come. To our Pueblo village of Isleta, he came riding upon a white horse. He came to help us. The padre was a good man. But we killed him and now he is dead."

Dozens of saddened villagers huddled around the priest's grave as misty rain fell from darkened skies. It was as if the angels from heaven above were also weeping for the beloved holy man. After dabbing his eyes and clearing his throat, Chief Dripping Water continued, "Father Padilla was always playing jokes and making us laugh. I remember the time he caught a trout and put it under my pillow; I never got him back for that stinky prank!"

Suddenly the earth rumbled. Kicking Bird shrieked and jumped to high heaven, as rocks covering Father Padilla's burial mound tumbled off his grave. Choking on the dirt bath, everyone coughed, wheezed, and rubbed watery eyes. And then, Father Padilla's big head burst through the earth, like an eager groundhog on the first day of spring! Next came one large, brawny hand and then the other. Fingers the size of sausages grasped at the embankment over his head, and he was gasping for air! His long, gray hair was tangled and bloodied as if he'd torn hunks of flesh from his scalp. His fingers were bloody, and his nails were scratched down to the quick. Those who hadn't already fainted or run away dropped to their knees in reverent prayer, while others dug with desperate hands. But once the holy man was pulled from his grave, they discovered that he was dead. Stranger still, the crude coffin split down the middle. Inside his brittle tomb were bloody scratch marks, proving that his effort to escape a dirt prison had been valiant. The next day, a sturdier casket was hewn from the trunk of a mighty cottonwood, and Father Padilla was entombed inside the chapel where he was buried under the pulpit.

Seven years later, parishioners entered the sanctuary one morning in early spring to find that the tree trunk had risen and was sticking out of the ground! Padre Padilla was on top of his coffin, lying under a thin layer of dirt. His arms were crossed over his chest, and a slight smile was frozen on the dead monk's face. Mysteriously, Padre Padilla's earthy remains were as fresh as a daisy.

Again Father Padilla had another burial. But seven years later, on a beautiful morning in early spring, his coffin resurfaced. Once again, he looked and smelled as pretty as a rose. After an examination, the restless corpse was reburied in a deeper grave, and seven years later, the earth over his grave began buckling.

Padre Padilla resurrects from his grave in Isleta every seven years. *Author's Collection.*

On August 28, 1894, the *Southwest Sentinel* declared: "Padre Padilla is rising to the surface of the ground for a fourth time. He is at Isleta, at the gospel beneath Saint Augustine."

Padre Anton Docher was summoned to hold an investigation. Sure enough, the coffin of Father Padilla had arisen and burst through the earth, for the fourth time in twenty-eight years! Along with several witnesses, the casket was reopened, and Padre Padilla looked to be resting in peace. Only a suspicious smile blemished the grim, austere expression frozen upon his face. During the postmortem examination, physicians noticed that Padilla was missing his sandals and his left foot. During the procedure, Padre Docher nicked his hand, and within days the wound became gangrenous. Doctors claimed that amputation of Padre Docher's arm was necessary to save his life. But the natives of Isleta invoked the supernatural powers of Padre Padilla to heal Docher, and his arm healed miraculously without surgery.

Before the restless monk was reburied for the fifth time, carpenters built a wooden floor to cover his grave. Over time, the miracles at Isleta were filed under an umbrella of miracles known as the "Rising Coffin of Padre Padilla," and the early riser was made into a martyr of the Catholic faith. But no matter what you choose to believe about this spooky legend, at least everyone can agree that Padre Padilla was a great man, and everyone knows that you can't keep a good man down, especially in the village of Isleta!

THE QUEEN'S HAUNTED MIRRORS

All is an Illusion.

—Buddha

Denver, Colorado, was once known as the Queen's City, for reasons that have long been forgotten. Except to an old-timer known as Fred Sturgis. Fred was a wildly entertaining fellow who never let truth get in the way of a good story. For many years, he enjoyed nightly company with familiar strangers at 1946 Market Street. After hanging his hat, he'd belly up to the serving board, order a frosty mug, and beg for an audience. Born with the gift of gab, he was especially fond of retelling historical ghost stories, likely because he was older than Methuselah and clearly understood the world of spirits. He'd obtained esoteric knowledge by going on astral journeys to exotic ports from Paris to Pluto.

One stormy night, Freddy took a sentimental trip down memory lane, and while staring into the bar-back mirror he fell into a psychic trance. His ancient body quaked, like an aspen tree, while his eyes bulged from sunken sockets. In a low, meditative voice he steadily hummed "OM . . ."

The new waitress at the Lodo Bar and Grill had never seen a serious spiritualist at work. After studying Fred's immaculate gaze, she demurred, "All is an illusion."

And with that truism, Fred broke from his entranced spell and fell into the green eyes of a smoldering Aphrodite. "Ella" was scrolled across her name tag, and Fred turned as white as the starched apron it was pinned on. After an awkward pause, he leaned forward on bent elbows and whispered, "You're the spitting image of my dearly departed love. My Ella was like Venus, that beguiling Romanesque sweetheart who stands in a colossal clamshell, whilst it arises from a frothy sea of foam. Ella will always be my stormy sea of green. But it was in the fault of our stars that our love was crossed . . .

"Our story began long ago, when Ella laid claim here. Not when this building served as a Buddhist temple, mind you, but when it first arose as a classy hotel. Although these hallowed halls became better known for harboring secrets than for alluring elegance . . . This building was erected at great cost by an astute businesswoman. Nobody knew where her vast fortune had come from. But nearly everyone called her Queenie because she stormed into Denver by surprise and soon became very wealthy. She reigned over Denver like it was her own, and it wasn't long before everyone was calling it the Queen's City! Believe it or not, this happy hellhole was once the finest mansion that anyone in this cowtown had ever seen. Four ominous faces are carved into the towering marble precipice, and the owner's angelic cameo graced the top, like Queen Bee. The three other mysterious mugs are of murdered politicians, who'd once stood in the queen's way. A rambling Masonic scroll rolls around the roofline along with other sacred symbols. Secret tunnels hollowed under the mansion allowed good ole boys to visit the gaming parlors without being seen by prying eyes. While discretion was the better form of valor, it still didn't keep crime at bay, and the neighborhood soon developed an unsavory reputation . . .

"The first time I visited the mysterious mansion happened quite by accident. I'd been walking home from the park when lightning bolts ripped through inky skies like daggers of fire thrown by an angry Zeus. Dark clouds opened and rain poured from the heavens. Since becoming an independent young man, my father always warned me not to ever leave home without a raincoat. I quickly realized that I'd picked a terrible night to rebel against his sound advice. It was late at night, and my parent's house was still two miles up a muddy country road. So, I dashed through several landscaped yards and found shelter under a pin-striped awning. My prayers were answered when a window opened from above and a girlish voice harkened, 'Welcome to the house of mirrors!' Happily I ran to the covered porch and rang a decorative brass bell. A massive door creaked open to a face slathered in cold cream. Introducing herself as the head housekeeper, her whisper reeked of wine and cigarettes. Softly she demurred that there weren't any vacancies, but I was welcome to sleep in the attic for free, in exchange for mowing her lawn. Without batting an eye, I accepted the generous offer. She smiled, patted me on the head like a puppy, and then pattered off to fetch another oil lamp.

"During her brief absence, I snooped around the shadowy side parlor. Being a farm boy, I'd never seen such a fine place. Each flash of lightning revealed a dazzling array of riches. Oil paintings of busty babes with ruby-red lips and pearly-white teeth smiled from gilded frames. Each beguiling angel floated over a sea of red-satin wallpaper flocked with velvet roses. Bronze statues of naked Grecian goddesses embellished every nook and cranny. Crystal chandeliers dangled from mirrored ceilings, and the silent touch of lamplight illuminated a symphony of rainbows. Once my guide returned and we meandered down darkened corridors. Every numbered door stood closed and all that could be heard was subdued laughter muffled by raging storm. Spicy incense tickled my nostrils, and I desired nothing more than a breath of fresh air. Windows were plenty, but all were suffocated by heavy, velvet curtains with dangling gold fringe. Two or three different shades layered over the glass to shutter sunlight. Plants must have died from starvation. Flowerpots held plump goldfish. Little dogs lounged about on satin pillows like Arabian sheiks, and each wore a sparkling collar that probably cost more than my parents' farm. There were twenty-seven rooms, which included four parlors, two kitchens, and a grand ballroom. Until that night, I'd never seen a flushing commode!

"From tower to cellar, the dazzling palace held dozens of gaudy mirrors, and all were precious gifts—given by a favored guest, a sea captain who sailed the seven seas. Priceless antiques, these exquisite mirrors were forged from precious diamond dust, and the secret to their making had been lost to the sands of time . . . Like Narcissus gazing into the pool at his own reflection, my tour guide couldn't stop admiring herself. Whenever we'd come upon a shiny mirror or bowl of fish, she'd stop to gawk at her pasty reflection. It was amusing, but I acted unaware of her bizarre obsession. Upon reaching the third floor, we walked a narrow passage that led to the attic staircase. My hostess handed me a cold skeleton key and warned that the lofty suite was haunted.

"Well, I didn't believe in such silly matters and was awfully tired. So I opened the door, and it slammed behind my heels, without warning. In the dim light, I stumbled up the musky staircase toward my lonely cell. Another door opened to a dusty chamber. A mahogany canopy bed draped by sky-blue curtains stood beneath an oil painting of Cupid grasping an arrow. A writing table hovered under a small window, and a potbellied stove sat burning coal in the corner. One wall boasted a huge, ornate mirror in the shape of an oystershell. The golden frame was engraved with smirking angels and menacing devils. I didn't care much for the primitive artwork, but the mirror itself was spellbinding. Flickers of radiant light danced in an ethereal pool, which appeared multidimensional and infinite. It was quite strange, and I was mesmerized. So, I made a mental note to learn more of the mysterious mirrors by seeking help at the Denver Public Library.

"After stripping off my soggy duds, I draped them over a corner sink and oozed between silky sheets. The fireplace flickered shadows across the ceiling, and rain pounded the rooftop. Suddenly, mystic smoke arose from the floorboards. I felt dizzy and seemed to fly out of my body. Off in the distance, a songbird sang in Chinese . . . only it sounded like I was listening from underwater. A while later, the clock chimed and my eyes bolted wide open. With a dry mouth and wet pillow, I wondered if I'd been dreaming. All I really knew in my convoluted state of mind was that I longed to be home, as heckling winds grew louder. I rolled over on my side and noticed a mysterious beam of pale moonlight, which fell through the lace-covered window and onto the oystershell mirror. As if entranced, I arose and stood naked before angels and demons. Mysterious images swirled in the looking glass. Several figures, the size of tiny dolls, gathered in a miniature replica of my attic chamber. I saw a shadowy woman wearing a transparent nightgown. With clenched fists she stood yelling at a dark figure.

"Suddenly, she raised a pistol to her temple and screamed, 'I'M HAPPY, OH SO HAPPY . . . I'M SO HAPPY THAT I'M GOING TO BLOW MY PRETTY HEAD OFF!'

"This mirage rippled away like restless waves upon a tranquil fishbowl, and then came another figure. A silver star was pinned to his chest, as he argued with a dark lady. The lawman grabbed her by the shoulders, shook her like a rag doll, and threw her into a rosewood curio cabinet. Glass shattered everywhere. A silver pistol was pulled from his pocket, and then the mystical mirror rippled into silent darkness. A man and then a woman screamed from downstairs, followed by deafening gunshots.

"I dashed back to my bed, pulled the curtains closed, and cowered under my covers, praying that the night would soon end. A few moments later, my chamber door creaked open and my heart pounded. A fallen angel parted sky-blue curtains and stood before me in a transparent white nightgown. She whispered in my ear, asking if I'd ever been to heaven. Her breath reeked of stale wine and cigarettes. I was confused. But she took me into her arms and made me believe in God. The sun rose as a cock crowed, and then that sweet angel of mercy kissed me goodbye.

"It continued to rain throughout that dreary day. Come to find out, I wasn't the only soul to experience loss of innocence that fateful evening. A milkman making morning deliveries died in that haunted house of horrors, while I lay sleeping under the wing of a dark angel . . . shot by a stray bullet, and I'd seen the tragedy unfold in the prophetic mirror, moments before it happened! But I couldn't tell anyone of my night in that palace of sin, lest I be called into the police station for questioning, and I didn't want trouble with the law, or my parents. So, I kept my lips sealed.

"The following week it rained every day, and by the time the grass finally dried, I'd forgotten about my ill-fated promise. But I never lost memory of being awakened by innocent love. Years slowly passed. I married, became a father, and owned a very successful business. The world was my oyster, and yet, I still wasn't happy. Then one lonely night, I fell under the dark spell of a familiar stranger. Only this time, she was reigning queen. Madame Ella Wellington had aged like a fine wine. I bragged that I'd made my fortune and had come back to give her a name and make her an honest woman. But she only demurred that her world was hers alone. I got down on bended knee and begged the green-eyed Venus to be my bride. But her senseless answer puzzled me.

"In a hypnotic daze, she arose from our love nest, parted sky-blue curtains, and praised, 'I'M HAPPY, OH SO HAPPY . . . I'M SO HAPPY THAT I'M GO-ING TO BLOW MY PRETTY HEAD OFF!' She'd become like a wild animal, with a crazed look in her eyes. She cried in a maddened frenzy, grabbed a look-ing glass, and then tossed her despised reflection heavenward! Like birds of a feather, slivers of quicksilver took flight! The vile vixen laughed manically while sobbing a river of tears. And random objects she threw in my general direction.

"I was plum flabbergasted. It was like being with Dr. Jekyll and Mr. Hyde . . . whenever she'd Jekyll . . . I'd hide! So, I ducked into the hallway and that's when the drama queen pulled a faithful trigger . . .

"The memory of Queenie's sweet love haunted me. I couldn't work. Nor could I eat. I became a mere shadow of the great man I once was. My nights were long and restless. So, I began sleeping on my beloved's fresh grave . . . But it was cold comfort. Three weeks after her untimely death, I drank a bottle of rat poison. My disgusted wife found my corpse. A withered photograph of my lovely Queenie I'd tucked inside a suicide note, pinned to my broken heart. My last request was that I be left where I died. So, on a stormy evening just like this one, I was buried, heart to heart and toe to toe with my lovely Ella . . . And that is where I still rest . . . during the day, anyway. At night, I'm always here, even if no one else is listening . . . Youth and beauty are fleeting treasures . . . All is an illusion . . ."

After taking a final swig of beer, Freddy gazed into the flickering mirror behind the bar back and winked at his transparent reflection . . .

Today's patrons of Denver's Lodo Bar and Grill claim the ill-fated lovers still haunt the former whorehouse turned Buddhist temple—and what's now a sportsman's watering hole. Could it really be Fred's and Ella's watery faces seen reflected in the bar-back mirrors . . . or is it all an illusion?

GHOST RIDERS OF LOCO GULCH

Money can't buy life.

—Bob Marley

In case you don't know, *loco* is a Spanish word meaning "crazy." Speaking of crazy, there's a wild yarn behind a ghost town by the name of Loco. It was situated on the dark side of a perilous mountain and on top of a desolate bed of the woolly locoweed. The pesky plant had an alluring fragrance and taste that attracted livestock like a moth to the flame. But once a beast dined on this sinister shrub, they couldn't stop. Locoweed addiction caused slow madness and death. Believe you me, there's nothing more terrible than watching an innocent heifer graze down that slippery slope. During the first stage of being "locoed," the cow craved only the loco plant and will eat nothing else. But ingesting this weed caused mania. The second stage was ushered in by sunken eyeballs, lusterless fur, and feeble movements. Locoed cows slowly starved themselves to death.

After learning about the dangers of locoweed, you might wonder why any sane person would try to build upon such deadly grounds. But once the cry of gold was heard, concerns over the deadly locoweed became secondary over hunger for riches. The second reason for naming the town Loco was because it's long been haunted! In fact, fear over a single ghost emptied the ill-fated town before paint was dry on the welcome wagon.

Professional ghost hunter Butch Baker was the first to meet the frightful phantom. It was back in the summer of 1863, during a hot night. It was so darn dry that a couple of bushes followed Butch's dog around, begging for a drink of water. And it was so darn hot that farmers fed ice cubes to chickens just to keep them from laying boiled eggs!

Upon a cloud of dust, Butch came riding into Loco. Leaking buckets of blood, he jumped from his horse, Elmer, in front of Tiny Tim's Saloon. He was exasper-

Butch Baker was the first loco ghost hunter known in Colorado.
Author's Collection.

ated and tried to warn fellow Locoans about the ghost he'd just encountered. So, his buddies carried him inside and propped his weary bones upon a proper barstool.

Once Butch had a steadied drink in hand, he whimpered, "I've been shot ... by a ghost!"

A few big-eared gamblers overheard his wild claim and began snickering over at the faro table. Butch may have been brave, but this insensitive gesture insulted his fragile ego. And so, he puffed up his chest and hollered, "I'm packing a set of pearly-handled Peacemakers that will surely argue against anyone who doubts my solemn word. I'm no coward, but I was just riding up in Georgetown County when a haunting scream caught my breath tight . . . I felt my skin crawl and my teeth chatter until I couldn't keep my darn mouth shut. My hoss, Elmer, began whinnying and bucking. He was fit to be boiled into glue . . . Suddenly I caught a whiff of burning sulfur and brimstone. And being a professional ghost hunter, as I am, I instinctively knew that spirits were in the mists. Then out of the darkness I spied a spooky figure swinging from the arm of a lofty cottonwood. With a pounding heart, I pulled my piece and crept closer. That's when I took notice of the bandito's hemp necklace. He was as white as a ghost and looked like he'd been dead for quite a spell. So, I reached up to relieve his pockets of any spare change, when he suddenly fluttered his eyeballs and hollered for help! In all my days, I'd never heard a ghost say anything more than BOO! I froze in my tracks. Quick as lighting, the ghoul pulled out a Bowie knife and cut himself down from the avenging noose. I couldn't believe my eyes! Then the terrible thing whipped out a gun from beneath his billowing burial robe and then floated toward me with the intent look of murder in his shifty eyes. But my sixth sense, along with the sight of the spook's six-shooters, told me the ghost hunt was over. So, I spurred ole Elmer, and we rode fast as the wind. But just as we came around the bend, I caught a lead pill in my leg. How that flighty phantom shot a moving target, I'm sure I don't know. Upon reaching the next ridge, I glanced behind and noted that we were being hotly pursued by a phantom horse and ghostly bandito! But I spurred Elmer over the ridge until we arrived in Loco!"

After spilling his guts at Tiny Tim's Saloon, nobody believed Butch's ghost story, until fellow barflies suddenly heard a horrible moan shoot up from the cellar. Jaws dropped from every pale face in the room. But being a brave ghost hunter, Butch hushed the worried crowd and assured them that he had everything under control. Silence was thicker than mud when a blood-curdling shriek suddenly shook the saloon from cellar to rafters.

Without thinking, Butch bolted for the door, but he quickly lost his balance and fumbled to the floor and then sputtered, "Why, that's the same holler that came from the phantom bandito . . . we'd better high-tail it out of here boys, because that evil spook won't take prisoners!"

Well, Butch didn't have to mention this sensible plan more than once, because within seconds, the dance hall, gaming tables, and bar had emptied. News of the ghost rider spread throughout Loco Gulch like wildfire. Horses were saddled, but the more impatient folks just hurried away on bareback. Hitched wagons scurried entire families away, pell-mell. Only one poor soul was left in the dust, and Butch knew he was a goner. But at least he had more guts than you could hang on a fence. So, he took a deep breath, pulled his gun belt over his chair, and prayed for a miracle.

Finally, the cellar door creaked open. A chalky white face followed a cocked pistol through the aperture. "Gotcha where I want ya!" yelped the ghost, and then he sassed,"This has been a fine day's work . . . robbing the entire town of Loco was easier than taking candy from a baby!" The intruder then poured a generous victory drink and helped himself to the faro dealer's forgotten money bag.

Weakly, Butch raised his head and feebly mumbled, "Who are you, phantom man, and why do you torment me so?"

But the interloper just chuckled and sneered, "Why, I ain't no ghoul! I'm Silver George from Mexico!"

As life slowly trickled from Butch's dying body, he summoned strength to whimper, "Aren't you a restless spirit from the great beyond?"

Before answering, the bandito tip-toed over and relieved Butch of his guns and wallet. Adding insult to injury, he also swallowed his last drop of beer. Silver George wiped his dripping mustache with the corner of a checked tablecloth, burped, and then chuckled, "Hell no, I'm not a ghost! I guess I fooled you with the white face paint and my impressive acting skills. I'm just as alive as you are, Butch Baker! But from the looks of things, you'll be joining the devil soon enough. Say hello to my friends in hell!"

Butch raised his head, and with his dying breath he humbly croaked, "Alas, the hunter has become the hunted. Damn you, forevermore, Silver George!"

Over the years, only one cowboy returned to Loco, and that was Silver George! In the afterlife, the vile bandito became a ghost rider! Legend tells us that night after night, a black stallion kicks trail dust into moonbeams as he storms through Loco Gulch. This frenzied phantom is chased by another ghost rider —Butch Baker! Colorado's first official ghost hunter never left Loco Gulch! On nights of the full moon, Butch Baker and his white phantom steed, Elmer, can still be seen galloping at breakneck speed, and only lightning hangs fire by comparison! Butch can also be heard screaming like a bat out of hell as he hunts for the brazen bandito in astral form. They say he's seeking revenge on the coward who stole his guns, his money, and his life! Not to mention his last swig of beer!

I suppose he'll never rest in peace until his death is avenged. Ghost hunting is a terrible addiction—once you start, you can never stop. And that's why most spooky people are considered loco. And speaking of crazy, not much remains of Loco except for its funny name and this laughable legend. But at least you've been warned about the phantom night riders of Loco Gulch and about being "locoed" on wacky weed!

MONSTERS OF THE LAKES

The deeper you go . . . the stranger it gets.

—Shark Week

In the Rocky Mountains there are more ancient lakes than can be counted, and Captain Clark knew then all. The salt of the earth, he'd been cruising the choppy waters of Bear Lake since he was knee high to a grasshopper. With a wind-burned face, he appeared much older than his years. Perhaps that's why he'd become known as the "Old Man of the Sea."

On August 6, 1953, Captain Clark was in an especially good mood. After clearing his throat, he bellowed, "If you all would please be seated, then we'll begin our relaxing tour around Bear Lake. This will be the final cruise of my long and illustrious career. My beloved wife of fifty years just passed over the Great Divide. So, I'm hanging up my captain's hat." A single tear streaked down his rugged cheek, which he quickly wiped away and sputtered, "See that spout over yonder? It reminds me of an old yarn about a fishermen who fell for a rich man's daughter. But the girl's father refused them to marry. So, the fishermen left to seek his fortune, but promised to return. A year later, he returned. As he sailed into the bay, he tooted the secret signal, which was three long blasts from the ship's foghorn. With a pounding heart his beloved jumped into the water and began swimming toward the boat. Once the fishermen sighted his sweetheart, he jumped into the water, eager to kiss her sweet lips. But a dense fog enveloped everything in their midst. In maddened desperation, they cried out for each other. But fate turned the spinning wheel of destiny, and they both drowned. However, the lovers were reunited at the bottom of the sea. So, whenever water sprays, it's the lovers dancing in eternal bliss! . . . Either that or it might be a sea monster.

"Don't believe me? Well, history teaches us much about what science fails to recognize. For example, 5,000 years ago, images of sea monsters were painted inside seaside caverns of the Pacific Northwest and along the South American

Monsters of the lakes have tormented the Rockies for many years.
Author's Collection.

coastline. It's interesting to note that although separated by thousands of miles, these similar paintings appear to be of an identical creature! In fact, one of the first written accounts about sea monsters was recorded in 1734. Explorer Hans Egede wrote in his log book that as his ship sailed past the coast of Greenland, a colossal sea serpent lifted its dragon-like head higher than the towering crow's nest! Its noodle-like body had *several* humps, and it stretched longer than the ship. The fearsome beast emitted an awful victory cry, which rattled the ship and its trembling crew. Its yawning mouth spit fire and incinerated several victims, before the monster sank into the murky depths.

"Sure, it might be easy to scoff at these ancient seafaring legends. But why not consider that there might be truth to these timeless tales? In fact, this might come as a big surprise, but several Rocky Mountain lakes are home to sea monsters.

"During the summer of 1864, a group of Mormon church elders, along with a conservative columnist from the *Desert Newspaper*, were cruising here at Bear Lake, when they sighted a humped-back beast silhouetted in the blazing sunset. The monster began swimming toward them and was close enough to touch before it sank beneath the water. And it wasn't long before there were copycat sightings. Folks in the Gem State told of a monster in Payette Lake, which locals called Slimy Slim, and of another unnamed beast at American Falls.

"Not to be outdone, folks in the Centennial State have long bragged of at least three sea monsters. Then, back here in the Beehive State, a fisherman spotted a sea monster swimming near the shores of Salt Lake. But that fish tale was taken with a grain of salt because the high mineral content of Salt Lake limited marine life.

"Certainly, Big Sky Country has had the most sightings. Especially at Flathead Lake. In 1889, Captain James Kerr was ferrying a steamboat loaded with awe-struck tourists, when they spied a sea serpent charging toward their boat. Fearing that the ship would be rammed, a quick-thinking passenger fired six rounds from his pistol. The brazen beast retreated, much to the relief of more than 200 wide-eyed passengers!

"Fear of the waters became epidemic. So, noted scholars gathered to discuss the problem. They concluded that the sea monsters could be a prehistoric fish species known as the 'Diabolo Dinothesium.' They surmised that these creatures were actually ancient dinosaurs that somehow survived the Ice Age and swam from lake to lake via subterranean channels. A full report of their findings was reported in the *Buena Vista Republican*. Why, even today sea monsters are still being sighted in the Rockies. Although they are rarely caught by fishing line or by camera."

Suddenly, the boat sputtered to a grinding halt! And a dozen unimpeachable witnesses watched in stunned silence as a huge wave suddenly washed Captain Clark overboard. Horrified passengers began screaming for their lives! It was pure bedlam. The SS *Minnow* was waterlogged and it began taking water when the second in command shouted: "Everyone into life boats!"

Thankfully, the sea monster never came back for dessert! Only one man perished—Captain Clark. Clark never made sainthood like his ancient predecessor, explorer Hans Egede. However, the Old Salt made history anyway, since his mysterious ill-fated retirement cruise was hard to forget.

Today, old-timers claim that the sea monster of Bear Lake is still spotted in those choppy waters, as is the ghost of Captain Clark. Local legend tells us that whenever water sprays from the depths of Bear Lake, it's the Old Man of the Sea . . . dancing with his beloved wife, throughout eternity.

DEATH SHIP OF THE PLATTE RIVER

A ship of death, which sails the sea
And is called *Carmilhan*
In tempests she appears
Without a helmsman she steers.

—Longfellow

They say the Platte River never forgets. But what it knows, nobody can remember. At least everyone agrees that it's haunted by a prophetic ship of death. And one of the first to witness this ominous watercraft was a ghost. Or so it seemed, when a dead man was pulled from the river and sputtered, "HELP!" In disbelief, the wide-eyed coroner stared down just as the corpse's eyes fluttered, and his teeth chattered, *"I'm n-n-n-n-not d-d-d-d-dead!"*

And then the baffled coroner stammered, "B-b-b-b-but why aren't you?"

And it was a darn good question. John Moran, also known as "Stuttering Jack," had been fishing along the Platte River when the so-called Ship of Death called him home. And Stuttering Jack wasn't the only victim of the evil ghost ship. Wyoming, the Cowboy State, has the most recorded accounts of death ship sightings, beginning with an old trapper known as Lucky Leon. The affable Frenchman once told reporters, "Yes, I've seen the Ship of Death and rue the day it happened. Back in 1862, my hunting party was trapping beaver along the Platte. Known as 'Black Gold,' beaver pelts were worth a fortune. We planned on working throughout the summer and then selling pelts in Saint Louis. The stakes were high in hostile Indian country. But we figured fast money was worth the risk. So we set up camp along a muddy stretch of the Platte River. Happily, we were soon stacking pelts and seeing dollar signs.

"Then one afternoon, I suddenly spotted a huge vessel sailing along the river. This was highly unusual as the muddy river couldn't support such a large craft. Stranger still, an ethereal haze was cast over the entire scene. I hollered for my buddies, and they saw her, too. Oddly, it appeared that the ship was floating

Rare photograph of the menacing Death Ship of the Platte River.
Author's Collection.

about a foot above the water's surface, as the hull and stern were clearly visible. Its decks projected beyond the hull, after the manner of an old Roman ship. There was a creaking and straining as if the barge had pushed against a stiff wind. Yet, the air was still. As the clipper emerged from an ethereal haze, billowing masts parted. Standing guard in the lofty crow's nest was a commandeering skeleton! The ghoulish skipper peered through a long and shiny brass looking glass and bellowed 'Come all ye wicked to the land of no return!' A skeleton crew of pirates danced about the deck, guzzling from tapped rum barrels and singing jolly ditties about the good ole days. One of the bony fiends held an hourglass, which he shook above his head like a tambourine while laughing manically. On the bow were a half-dozen ghouls huddled together, and they took turns painting on an easel.

"Once the ship drew closer, freakish artists held up a large canvas, and I'll be damned if it wasn't a portrait of my beloved fiancé! I squinted to get a better look. But then the ghost ship vanished into thin air!

"Afterwards, we never said a word . . . as if not mentioning the ship would somehow erase it from memory. That evening we were sitting around a toasty campfire, enjoying a hearty dinner of pan-fried trout, when strange noises emanated from the nearby riverbank. Once again, we endeavored to ignore the peculiar phenomenon. But it wasn't easy. So, we turned to our bedrolls and hoped for merciful sleep. I snored like a log until whispering between the others awakened me. The boys were frightened because they'd heard strange sounds coming from the nearby river. But I couldn't hear a darn thing, save for the cry of a lonesome wolf. So, I proclaimed to be an authority on such matters as haunted waters. And I reassured my cowardly pals that the river was noisy because it contained moving gas, just as my stomach was doing after our hearty, late-night supper. To illustrate my point, I administered a foul noise of my own making and then pardoned myself with a half-hearted grumble. My transparent reassurance made them giggle like a bunch of schoolgirls. And so it was that they began happily chatting about the future. Two of the boys planned on buying a saloon, and the other dreamed of opening a brothel. But I wanted only peace and quiet, and so I doused the lantern, saying it was time to get some shut-eye.

"But we tossed and turned while suffering through terrifying nightmares. Haunting screams awoke us all at once. Not a single word was spoken as we lay under a blanket of stars, trembling in fear. For hours, we listened to the terrifying din cut through the awkward silence. And yes, it sounded like a vessel was drawing near upon the water. When the light of dawn finally reached over the horizon, we spied smoky mists arising from the river, and the Ship of Death was drifting toward the nearby shoreline.

"We broke camp so fast that lightning hangs fire by comparison! And it wasn't until we'd reached Cherry Creek that we remembered our forgotten fortune. Black gold! For a split second the others considered returning for their hard-earned treasure. But I put my foot down, insisting that I was an authority on such matters as escaping from haunted rivers. I advised that it was smart to leave the beaver pelts behind as a token offering to the watery underworld for sparing our lives. That sound logic made perfect sense to the others. And so we hastened home, hoping to put the haunted horror behind us. But that was not to be. Because after arriving in Saint Louis, I learned that my fiancé had suddenly expired. No doubt, I'd been cursed by the ship of ghouls!"

Still another sighting of the Death Ship occurred in 1887, when a half-dozen cattlemen spotted the ship. Just like before, partying skeletons guzzled rum while a busy crew painted mysterious canvases. Once the painting was revealed, it showed one of the men's brothers. And it was soon learned that the rancher's brother had died at the same moment the painting was presented.

Then, in 1918, a soldier driving horses outside Fort Laramie spied the ghost ship. His frightened team jumped into the river and drowned. Moments later, the soldier was also dead, zapped by a random bolt of lightning that came from the clear blue sky! Coincidence? I think not! The *Denver Post* didn't think so, either. Especially since their lead reporter was none other than Stuttering Jack. After being rescued from the Denver morgue, Jack became a ghost expert for the newspaper, and front-page news was never the s-s-s-same!

FOUNTAIN OF LOVE

It costs a great deal to be reasonable. It costs youth.

—Madame de la Fayette

Everyone has heard of the fabled Fountain of *Youth*, which remained elusive to Ponce de Leon. But do you know of the Fountain of *Love*? For many years, this sacred watering hole was known only to the native Utes. Then, in the late 1800s, a peaceful community called "Love" blossomed near the holy spring. But nobody in Love was aware of its magical spring water until a mighty Ute chieftain came along. After sharing a peace pipe with the mayor of Love, Chief Long Spear and Mayor Beard became fast friends.

Mayor Beard learned that the chieftain's secret to youth and longevity came from drinking sacred waters. Beard was skeptical, but curious. So, he dipped his tankard into the bubbly waters along Beaver Creek and drank his belly full. Lo and behold, the next morning he looked in the mirror and smiled at the face of a much-younger man! So, Mr. Beard happily traded three cows for sipping rights and promised that only he would drink from the sacred hole.

So, at the foot of Cow Mountain, where antelope played in green meadows and tweety birds sang sweet love songs, Mayor Beard established a dairy farm. Within a year, fat and happy heifers were producing creamy bovine juice that was sweeter than clover honey. Beard was making milk money hand over fist. That is, until Chief Long Spear spied thirsty cows guzzling from the sacred spring! Soon thereafter, Beard's herd produced only buttermilk. The befuddled dairy farmer went to the mighty chieftain and begged for forgiveness. Three more cows were given to Long Spear, and it wasn't long before creamy sweet milk was again forthcoming.

One sunny day, Mayor Beard invited chums over for a swim. Everyone went skinny dipping in the magic spring. Like heathens worshipping at the shrine of Bacchus, their debauchery was shameless! Chief Long Spear came along and witnessed the violation of sacred waters. The next morning, all of Mr. Beard's

Mr. Beard abused the Fountain of Love, which led to ruin.
Author's Collection.

cows were found dead without apparent cause. Being mayor and all, he was understandably furious. Needless to say, it's utterly impossible to run a dairy farm without udders. Beard realized his livelihood was at stake. But he wasn't willing to give up on his halcyon dreams. So he went to the library, hoping to find an answer.

Lo and behold, he overheard a knowledgeable bookworm whispering about the king of Spain. Apparently, his royal highness had seven dazzling daughters. But he hoped for snakes and snails and puppy dog tails. In other words, his majesty was desperate for a male heir. Mr. Beard surmised that the mystical waters of Love might help the royal family. So he sent a bottle of Love's bubbly spring water to Spain and hoped for the best. Low and behold, just nine months later, the Spanish queen produced a bouncing baby boy!

The king was mighty grateful. So, he sent a thoughtful thank-you note along with a bottle of sherry and a smoked ham, but the king still refused to invest in Mayor Beard's ailing dairy farm.

Then one fine day, Mr. Beard noticed that his baby boy was already sporting chest fur, and he suddenly realized that the miracle water also fostered hair growth! News about the miraculous waters of Love spread like wildfire! When Mr. Beard was interviewed by newspapers, he winked at a pretty reporter and bragged about having more giddy-up in the bedroom than a man half his age!

Mayor Beard knew he'd make a fortune by milking the waters of Love. So he went to work on a marketing plan. Advertising posters for Love Miracle Tonic depicted the sexy centurion Chief Long Spear in all his manly glory. He was shown rippling with muscles and long, black illustrious hair. Surrounding the chieftain was an army of pretty wives and handsome sons. But when Chief Long Spear saw the flashy posters, he was again angered and trouble soon followed. The *Aspen Daily Times* was quick to report these problems. One article described how two men and a woman were drinking the waters of Love, when they were suddenly and inexplicably sucked into the heavens! And the *Globe Democrat* reported that Mr. E. C. Perry witnessed guzzling cows being whisked into the clouds! Within months, many more unsuspecting citizens disappeared after drinking from the sacred spring, including the local minister. Beard, went on a fact-finding mission and learned that famed science fiction writer Ambrose Bierce also vanished after drinking sacred spring water. Word about the freakish waters spread like wildfire, and anyone with half a brain pulled up their tent stakes and moved to greener pastures.

Today, all that remains of the old ghost town is its romantic name. Yet, a few old-timers in the know still sip from the sacred hole. But thankfully, nobody has been vaporized, lately. And that's because the spring's hidden location is now a well-guarded secret. So, if you ask locals in Teller County where to drink from the Divine Cup . . . I guarantee they'll look at you like you're crazier than a one-eyed bedbug! But I'll give you a few hints . . . the sacred spring of Love can still be found at the foot of Cow Mountain, where the grass grows thick on mossy banks of Beaver Creek. Look for antelope romping in green meadows and listen for tweety birds singing sweet love songs. Keep in mind that those lucky few who sip from the sacred hole are easily recognized by their youthful step, furry faces, and sweaty palms.

QUEEN OF THE DAMNED

Any excuse will serve a tyrant.

—Aesop

A cursed lake of the Medicine Bow Mountains has remained haunted since times of yore. Long known as the "Lake of Hate," its unpleasant name was eventually changed to the friendlier-sounding "Lake Hattie." But this change has done nothing to appease the angry spirits who still dwell beneath those dark waters.

One of the first ghost stories about the lake began in October 1891. Bigwigs from the Wyoming National Bank played hooky from work by going duck hunting, and that was the last time anyone ever saw them. It was inexplicable why their boat capsized, because it was warm that fateful afternoon. Both men were avid outdoorsmen, sailors, and swimmers. Their vessel was found in good mechanical condition. But deep scratches that ruined its fresh paint and scattered feathers suggested that the watercraft had been attacked by a flock of violent birds! Adding to the puzzle, the victims' bodies weren't recovered, and without corpses the mystery couldn't be solved.

A team of professional deep-sea divers from San Francisco did an investigation for the whopping price of $15,000. But after a tedious month of dragging murky depths, frogmen pulled up their nets. Winter set in and the lake froze solid, but loved ones still refused to give up the ghost. The nation's top spiritual mediums meditated over the lake for countless hours. However, nothing resurfaced—not a coat, hat, or shoe. After two tiresome months of searching in vain, loved ones finally threw in the towel.

Word spread about the strange mystery, and it was soon learned that the Cheyenne Indians possessed secret knowledge about the mysterious lake. Chief Running Bear is recalled to have said: "Those two men you are looking for will never be found. Lake of Hate never gives up her dead. My people have good reason to shun those haunted shores. A wicked queen of the damned dwells in a subterranean cave. Nobody knows how she came to live in the underwater lair

The Queen of the Damned is a mysterious bird-woman
who lives in Lake Hattie and thrives on human sacrifice!
Author's Collection.

or for how long it's been her home. But for many moons, my people have thrown
captives into those waters as human sacrifice. She takes all men who come her
way, but her carnal lust can never be completely satisfied. Over the years, she's
become mistress over an army of dead lovers.

"Only two brave souls have seen the elusive queen and lived to tell about it.
The first was an Indian brave who was hunting near the lake when he spied a
beautiful woman swimming. She sang the most-mesmerizing songs he'd ever
heard. He fell in love with the mysterious maiden, but he dared not move or his

secret hiding place would be discovered. Suddenly, the bathing beauty turned to look in his direction and caught him by surprise. She had lovely wings of a bird, but the vile face of a viper! Had the Indian brave just kept the accidental discovery a secret there would have never been trouble. But what he saw was much too terrible to keep quiet. The next morning the brave hunter was found dead. Wrapped around his throat was an enormous rattlesnake.

"After finding the dead warrior, the Cheyenne chieftain was unafraid. He boasted that he was much wiser than the foolish Indian brave, and thus his tribe enticed him to challenge the vile viper queen. So, a medicine man gave the chief a magic shirt and sacred talismans that would protect him against her ominous powers. On the night of the dark moon, the brave chief pushed his canoe away from the shoreline, as his people cheered and wished him luck. Once at the center of the lake, he spied the mysterious woman swimming toward him. She began calling his name and hypnotizing him with maddening melodies. Playfully she rocked the boat and giggled while splashing him with water. But the chief thwarted her devious efforts by throwing magic stones. The sorceress grew angry and called upon the wild fowl to destroy the warrior! Clouds parted to release legions of angry eagles, hawks, and falcons, which flew at him from every direction! They beat his head with their powerful wings, pecked out his eyes with sharp beaks, and scratched his skin with mighty talons. But the forceful fowl couldn't throw the mighty warrior overboard. Undaunted, the Queen of the Damned called upon her army of dead soldiers, who resurrected from the depths and swam toward the canoe. But the chief back-paddled toward the shoreline as this unholy guard quickly followed in hot pursuit. Once reaching safety, he peeled off his magic shirt and lay down in the canoe to rest. That's when an undercover snake slithered from beneath a blanket and bit the prideful chief on the nose!"

Chief Running Bear took a contemplative drag from his peace pipe and continued his story by saying, "After the great chieftain died, nobody ever challenged the lusty lady of the lake. But when pioneers rolled into the region faster than they could be counted, my people used the snake woman's insatiable appetite to our great advantage. I recall that the white man's calendar told that it was in November of 1853. A large party of pioneers were on their way over the mountains, headed to a distant land called Oregon, when Cheyenne soldiers surrounded their wagons and held them in a snow-covered meadow. Held there as prisoners, the argonauts set up camp and hoped reinforcements from nearby Fort Bridger would soon come to their rescue.

"Days slowly passed. Then one morning they awoke to a thundering alarm! Once stepping from wagons and onto soggy grounds, the pioneers realized that they'd been intentionally forced to camp upon a snow-covered lake! Within seconds, men, women, children, horses, and oxen sank into oblivion, and the Queen of the Damned swallowed them all. And yes, the vile snake woman still hungers for victims! And even today, the queen of the damned still swallows disagreeable tourists . . . Know that you've been warned!"

SIZZLING GARNET

If you play with fire, you're going to get burned.
—Unknown

The truth may surprise you, but there are more cases of people exploding in the Rocky Mountains than anywhere else on the planet. Spontaneous human combustion occurs in high altitudes, when the body self-ignites and burns like a campfire marshmallow. Although there is no smoke, temperatures reach thousands of degrees Fahrenheit and instantly incinerate the body to ash within seconds. Spontaneous human combustion is often fatal. But not always. Take for example the case of drunken Jack the Lumberjack, of Harlem, Idaho. The rotund drunkard suffered terribly from aches and pains. So, doctors advised drinking a thimble full of kerosene oil every evening in order to relieve his aggravating symptoms. One night he was drinking a wineglass full as he lusted over the girlie section of the Sears, Roebuck and Company's catalog, when suddenly a blue ribbon of flames leapt from his lips to his loins! Thank goodness he had the presence of mind to close his mouth and shove fingers up his nostrils, since this cautionary act suffocated the flames and saved his life! On January 27, 1881, the Idaho statesman applauded the lumberjack for his quick thinking.

Yet, not everyone has been so fortunate. Consider the presentation of Mrs. Taylor, of Boise, Idaho. For many years, the chubby granny lived alone in peace. Then one day, her neighbor detected a foul odor seeping from her cabin. Police broke down the door and found the oldster deader than a coffin nail. She'd been sipping a glass of sherry while reading a steamy romance novel when she suddenly exploded. At least she didn't suffer. Her feet were all that remained of her, and they were still wearing fluffy, pink slippers. Of course, oldsters die every day. But not like this. Nothing in Mrs. Taylor's home suffered from flames or smoke. Yet, a greasy, black residue stuck to the ceiling and coated her recliner. Over the years, a nauseating odor lingered in the cabin, as did Mrs. Taylor's stinky ghost!

Happy Chappy became the toast of Garnet before he was toasted.
Author's collection.

In Michael Harrison's 1976 bestselling book titled *Fire from Heaven*, the author notes that poltergeist activity always results after someone suddenly explodes, and it's no wonder why! One of the most intriguing ghost stories about exploding people concerns Chester Chatterley. Better known as Happy Chappy, the wealthy Englishman lived a clean life by going to church every Sunday. He read from the good book and washed his hands before every meal. Food was Chappy's only solace, and over time he became all he'd swallowed. Doctors warned he'd die if he didn't change his eating habits. So, to start life anew, Chappy moved away from his old stomping grounds. During the long journey to the Montana Territory, he had plenty of time to pray and contemplate his future. Once he arrived in the mining town of Garnet, he took a deep breath of fresh alpine air and decided that he'd live like there was no tomorrow! His first stop was the Garnet Saloon, where he toasted the town with his very first beer. Over time his deep pockets drew barflies, like bees to honey, and Chappy became the life of every party. On one drunken spree, he smoked an opium pipe and married a Chinese prostitute who was young enough to be his granddaughter! But before the ink was dry on their marriage license, his new bride left after discovering her groom was already married. When Chappy's first wife learned of his deceitful two-timing, she divorced him, too. But despite bigamy, drunkenness, and gambling, he was as happy as a clam. Especially after losing five pounds with a new energy drink called "Cocaine Cola."

One fateful night, the oldster returned from a Chinese brothel known as the House of False Affection, drunker than a monkey. So the hotel housekeeper helped him to his chamber. As she fluffed pillows, Chappy slumped down in a comfortable chair and watered his tonsils. Upon seeing the busty babe silhouetted in the incoming moonlight, inspiration struck. In the twinkling of an eye, the old man wobbled toward his pretty prize with open arms and unzipped britches. But once the young maiden was within desperate reach, the dirty old man burst into a pillar of flames! The maid screamed to high heaven as the human torch staggered over to the window and crashed through the glass! Ear-piercing death cries consumed the still night air as the old man plummeted and then splattered onto Main Street. Although Chappy was not a smoker, his smoldering ashes suggested otherwise. The bucket brigade doused the sputtering sparks and swept away diminutive remains. A thorough investigation of the stinky situation revealed that the fat man's entire body was incinerated. The preacher said a passing prayer over the grease spot, and the doctor determined that Chappy's explosion was caused by gluttony and lust. Residents of the mining hub were aghast at the tragedy and did their best to dismiss the horrible affair. But the weird incident was hard to forget. The odor of burnt meat often wafted through the streets, and screams of terror echoed throughout town. Gruesome ghost stories swirled, and Garnet developed an unsavory reputation.

Today, Happy Chappy still haunts the old ghost town. Surely he's not the only restless spirit. But he is the only one that smells like burnt meat. Incidentally, paranormal investigators agree that Garnet is the most haunted ghost town in the Rockies. Why? It's because of quantum physics, my friends. In the fascinating book *Ghost Hunting in Colorado*, author Clarissa Vazquez is quoted as saying, "Quartz . . . can be utilized in radio and radar transmissions. Under the right conditions, it can produce electrical charge (piezoelectricity) and transmit ultraviolet light waves better than glass. It has the physical capacity for retaining light energy that could possibly result in a residual haunting."

Since the town of Garnet is built upon quartz, the prolific hauntings make perfect sense. So, it seems that Garnet is doomed to remain haunted. But what's a ghost town without ghosts anyway?

So, if you live in the Rocky Mountains or plan on visiting anytime soon, please take the doctor's advice. In order to avoid risk of exploding at high altitudes and becoming a sad ghost, you'll need to refrain from gluttony and lust. Of course, this may not be easy. But it could save you from spending eternity in the Rockies.

SPIRITS OF THE MERRY WIDOW

The drunkard's joy is the sober man's woe.

—Unknown

Today, the Merry Widow Health Mine is better known for curing than for killing. Sicklings pay a nominal fee to sit in the defunct mining tunnels and soak up residual radiation. Health seekers claim that taking carcinogenic air baths cures them of their nagging health ailments. But long ago, the mine was a dangerous operation where many employees died from horrible accidents. So, it's no wonder why the deadly mine turned health resort has seen its fair share of ghosts.

The Merry Widow was a fiery redhead who had the dubious distinction of being meaner than a Gila monster. I guess you could say that she never took crap from anybody. She'd inherited the gold mine after her hubby was found dead in a swanky hotel room along with his much-younger mistress. And that's when the ghost stories began. Jack Jasper recalled the tragedy while he nervously waited in the manager's office. After a shift bell sounded, the Merry Widow strutted inside and slammed the office door behind her, making the glass fearfully shutter in its pane. Wearing a slinky, crimson-colored gown over black combat boots, her classic features were faultless: tall and slim with long, tangled red hair that hung over her shoulders like a fiery shawl. And a fat stogie dangled from her painted scarlet lips as she hissed, "Just yesterday morning, a drilling man was blown into eternity . . . You'll be taking Brian's place . . . A drilling man works alone, much like a castaway adrift at sea. It's a lonely and dangerous job. A premature explosion filled the tunnel with smoke, and Brian couldn't get out in time. Until the day he died, the deadbeat always blamed supernatural forces for his ineptitude. Last week, the sniveling drunkard pulled the emergency bell, saying that a gang of tommy-knockers had beat him up and stole his liquid lunch. Like I'd believe in devilish elves stealing his jar of tonsil varnish. And Boozy Brian also claimed that barking hellhounds chased him throughout the underworld. Still another whopper was about a towering goat that walked on hind legs and had balls of fire for horns. The drunkard claimed that this hideous beast galloped

Rare photo of a ghost chasing a frightened miner
from the Merry Widow Mine. *Author's Collection.*

throughout the tunnels, with flashing red eyes, and his incessant bleating sounded like thunder. Come to think of it, the drilling man before Brian was another boozehound with the same old song and dance. God rest the soul of Whiskey Willy . . . Perhaps it takes liquid courage to be a drilling man. Alas, the drunkard's joy is the sober man's woe . . . Well, good luck and be careful of evil spirits!"

Jack thanked the Merry Widow and then jumped into the ore bucket. Once the hoisting bell sounded, the vessel plunged down the mining shaft. His heart raced as his stomach turned somersaults. After sinking 300 feet, the vessel shrieked to an abrupt stop. As the bucket swayed in the dark shaft, it was dead quiet. Suddenly, icy breath tickled the back of his neck and a women's voice whispered, "DEATH COMES!"

Rose perfume permeated the still air as goose bumps sprouted over his shivering hide. Jack took a deep breath and recalled another story he'd heard about the former owner and his secret mistress. The coroner ruled they'd both died from a stomach ulcer. Seemed unlikely since they'd died in bed together. But nobody would argue with the doctor, who happened to be a friend of the Merry Widow's.

Ever since their suspicious deaths, word around the grapevine told that the mine was haunted. But Jack didn't want to think about ghosts, and so he was relieved when a rapid rumbling indicated that the problem was fixed. A horn sounded and the pulley rope jolted. Again the eager vessel plunged downward. After sinking another 300 feet, the ore bucket screeched to a jerking halt. Jack scampered out and stretched his long legs. Through the looming darkness he wandered by candlelight until finding his new work station. Into hard granite he drilled. Holes were filled with gunpowder, and then he set each aperture with a long fuse. It was a wet tunnel; walls and ceilings dripped with condensation. After mopping sweat from his brow, he packed a corncob pipe with cherry tobacco. As sweet smoke swirled around his hat, he began thinking again of the woman's haunting presence and feared encountering the Merry Widow's most infamous phantom: the murdered mistress. He'd heard how she was often seen wearing a flowing funeral gown and was heard singing with terrible woe. Whenever she'd call a miner by name, death always followed.

Again, Jack shuddered in fear. All was silent save for the nagging torment of dripping water. Suddenly a measured ringing of a striking hammer joined the cacophony. As if beckoned by an unseen force, Jack tramped toward the mysterious sound. He then climbed up to a ledge and raised the candle above his head, while searching the yawning darkness with strained eyes. But the hope of light couldn't be seen. Splashing water drew closer.

With a pounding heart, he hastened toward the intruder, shouting: "Hey, is anybody there?"

Drip . . . drip . . . drip was his only reply.

"Is this some kind of an initiation joke? Well, I'm not laughing. Who are you? What do you want? Answer me, you damn coward!"

Again, the miner could hear swishing footsteps, followed by snarling dogs. His heart pounded as a dismal candle slipped from trembling fingers. In blinding darkness, he fumbled to light another. But the match fell into muddy water. In desperation, he hugged granite walls and guided himself through harrowing darkness. Barking dogs drew closer as Jack's trembling fingers yanked on a cold wire, which signaled the top-side station. After jumping into the ore bucket, Jack arose to the surface.

"What the hell is your problem?" demanded his red-faced boss.

"It . . . It . . . it happened," stuttered Jack.

The Merry Widow raised penciled brows and gave him a knowing look, saying, "tommy-knockers, girlie ghosts, or hellhounds?"

Jack nodded his head in agreement, licked quivering lips, and stammered, "Yes . . . yes . . . yes . . . I've never been so frightened in my life!"

But his boss snarled, "To anyone who works alone in the dark, strange sounds can emblaze a man's imagination. But there's always a logical explanation. Like when the timber-framed braces grow rotten and break with a snap. The terrible crash can reverberate throughout the tunnel, and it can sound like singing, laughing, or whispering. And sometimes empty chambers collapse and send tumbling clouds of dust through smothering passageways. This is how candles are extinguished and lunch buckets are lost. Remember that this is the age of reason, my good man. Ghosts can't hurt you. But if you're frightened, then try banishing them before getting scared and walking off the job. The best way to lay ghosts is to outsmart them. Disguise yourself, so they won't recognize you. You can do this by turning your clothes inside out and wearing them backwards. And if you see a spirit, walk backwards with your eyes closed. If you act like you can't see them, then they'll think they're invisible. And lady ghosts abhor foul odors. So, why don't you rub a wet meadow muffin over your trembling hide? That should do the trick. No more freakish phantoms and Jack Jaspers doesn't get fired!"

After the sharp tongue lashing, Jack was embarrassed for behaving like a sniveling schoolgirl, especially in front of a woman. So, the next morning, he went back to his work station with a refreshed attitude. Around noon, he'd just finished drilling holes, and before lighting the fuses he patrolled the tunnel, making certain it was clear of obstructions.

Suddenly, a beautiful woman with flowing locks of auburn hair floated before him! She tried to gain his attention by waving her wispy arms in frantic warning. The drilling man fumbled backwards and everything went dark . . .

Upon discovering Jack's lifeless body at the bottom of a shaft, the Merry Widow spat a wad of brown chew and sneered, "A corkscrew will never pull a drunkard from a hole!"

Jack's overalls were turned inside-out and he was wearing them backwards. Inside his pocket was a farewell letter. Scrawled in blood was his dying message: EVIL SPIRITS. He also smelled like fresh crap. Ironically, Jack Jasper wasn't a drinking man. However, he was a nervous fellow and obviously not well suited to be a drilling man. And the Merry Widow? Well, she never took crap from anybody.

33

ROGUE OF RAWLINS

I'm not afraid of death; I just don't want to be there when it happens.

—Woody Allen

A pair of human nipples haunt the Carbon County Museum in Rawlins, and I'll bet you're dying to know why. This all started with a gang of misfit bandits known as the Simms Gang. Like the infamous Jessie James Gang or the Wild Bunch, these notorious outlaws robbed trains. Only the Simms Gang wasn't any good at being bad. George Parrott was the most recognizable gang member. He bragged of being the infamous outlaw Jesse James. But nobody ever believed his wild claim, since Parrott's huge beak was impossible to disguise. In 1878, the bumbling bandits bungled a train robbery, and their ineptitude ended in the death of two affable lawmen. Wanted posters depicted Parrott's enormous nose and shouted a whopping $20,000 reward for anyone who captured the walking proboscis, dead or alive. Three years later, Parrott was flying low in the Big Sky Country when he got drunker than a fiddler's clerk and squawked about his dirty deeds. The astute saloonkeeper recognized Parrott's beak and called the sheriff. George was arrested and ordered to stand trial in Rawlins. At the Rawlins jail, Parrott pled guilty and found religion. Even after swearing he was a changed man, George was sentenced to dance with the hangman.

While awaiting execution, the resourceful bandit used a stiff nose hair to pick a tempting lock, and an open window was his last chance for freedom. But before making his great escape, nature called with a case of the runs, and so he dashed into the water closet for quick relief. Moments later, the jailbird was caught with his pants down. News spread about Parrott nearly flying the coop, and this sent a crowd to the mayor, crying for justice. But he turned a deaf ear, saying that justice would be served through proper legal process.

Late that night, vigilantes stormed George's jail cell. The avengers lassoed Parrott by his beak and dragged their prisoner kicking and squawking all the way to steely railroad tracks. By sunrise, an angry mob of over 200 citizens had gath-

ered, demanding a show. While calling for Jesus, George climbed upon an awaiting pickle barrel. An avenging hemp necklace dangled from a towering telegraph
pole and was tightened around a gulping Adam's apple. On the count of three,
the executioner kicked the barrel away, leaving the prisoner to swing like a crazed
piñata!

As George kicked, the nagging noose slipped upward until a final jolt sliced
off his ears. One flew to the east and the other to the west. But both sailed like
freebies over a roaring crowd. Parrott's left ear landed in a baby carriage. A teeth-
ing babe caught the ear with an open mouth and gleefully sucked upon its hairy
lobe. The right ear fell atop a picnic basket, and a wiener dog gobbled the happy
prize. Once again the crowd rallied with excitement.

Parrott struggled to his feet and tried to run away, but ankle irons rendered
the jailbird pigeon-toed. (At least the earless prisoner couldn't hear the crowd
mocking his feeble attempts at freedom.) George cried for his mommy and begged
to be shot, but the hangman shook his black hood in blunt refusal. On their second try at flipping the bird, Parrott was forced to climb a tall ladder while wearing ankle shackles. Of course the jailbird fumbled, but the crowd waited patiently until the prisoner was properly perched. Once again, the rope hissed to a
short drop. George's twitching body cast a grotesque shadow upon the blood-thirsty
audience, and it looked like a dark phantom doing a midair wizard dance. Revelers counted aloud with each passing swing of the dark pendulum . . . 10 . . . 11
. . . 12 . . . On the thirteenth swing Parrott untied his wrists, grabbed the telegraph
pole, and flew to an upper crossbeam! Hanging upon the wooden cross, Parrott
prayed aloud for another miracle. A heckling audience cackled as George's
knuckles blanched white as snow.

A drunkard shouted, "Hey Georgie Boy, can you give me a helping hand?"
While another jeered, "How's the weather up there, Parrott Beak?" But their
insults only fell on Parrott's fallen ears. After about five torturous minutes, ten
reluctant fingers uncurled, one by one. For the third time a crazed bird flew over
a giddy crowd. As the drop-jawed audience gawked, Parrot's dark form ebbed in
ever-diminishing arcs until his shadow danced no more. He'd been satisfacto-
rily jerked to Jesus. Adding insult to injury, George's stiffening corpse hung from
the telegraph pole, as tapped wires sent word down the line that the dreadful
Parrott was dead. Furthermore, the outlaw's lifeless body was left to hang for
several days as a gruesome reminder that crime never paid. In the Old West,
pioneer justice was never served cold.

It became the city's responsibility to bury George. But the undertaker couldn't
nail down the coffin lid because of Parrott's offending beak. So, they turned him
face down, but the lid wouldn't close over the coffin. The undertaker refused to
make a bigger coffin, and so he sawed off Parrott's head. A plaster death mask
was made from his earless face. George's brain was dissected by physicians interested in studying the criminal mind. His skull became the property of Wyoming's
first female doctor, and she used the trophy as an ashtray. Parrott's skin went to
a tannery in Denver, where it was pounded into fine Italian leather and fashioned

into a matching pair of oxfords. Specific instructions indicated that George's large, pink nipples were to be centered onto the toe of each dress shoe. Being impressed with his new human-skinned, nipple-toed oxfords, Dr. Osborne flaunted them everywhere, saying they brought him good luck. After winning the close election for Wyoming governor, Osborne boasted about winning by the *skin of his shoes*. A doctor's bag and coin purse were also fashioned from George's fine flesh, and Osborne relished in showing off these macabre trophies.

For many years, the nipple-toed Oxfords stood in a glass trophy case in the lobby of the Rawlins National Bank. But, the human skin shoes got the boot after being replaced by the preacher's stuffed Siamese calf. Then, in 1950, horrified construction workers unearthed a pickle barrel overflowing with putrid body parts. Historians recalled the gruesome story and gave a name to the human stew. Bones were fished from the barrel. The lower half of Parrott's skull went to the Union Pacific Railroad Museum in Council Bluffs, Iowa. But nobody knows what's happened to the human-skinned medicine bag and matching coin purse. Perhaps these crispy keepsakes will one day make a surprise appearance on *Antiques Roadshow*. Today, the nipple-toed Oxfords are on permanent display at the Carbon County Museum in Rawlins. Although without benefit of shoe polish, the pink tips have lost their youthful hue, and this is why they still haunt the Rawlins Museum! Stranger still, mysterious footsteps can always be heard throughout the museum, even when nobody is around. Perhaps the Rogue of Rawlins is still trying to make his final great escape . . . even if its by the skin of his nipple-toed shoes!

BIGFOOT OF BISHOP MOUNTAIN

As we acquire more knowledge, things do not become more
comprehensible but more mysterious.

—Albert Schweitzer

Do you believe in Bigfoot? This mysterious creature is an elusive apelike homi-
noid species that secretly thrives in remote, mountainous regions. Modern-day
scientists have deemed Bigfoot as being nothing more than a mythical monster.
But since ancient times, this beast-man has been known throughout the world.
In Asia he's feared as the "Yeti." In Europe, he's called the "Abdominal Snow-
man." Natives of North America had hundreds of different names for this elusive
creature, including Mat Log and Devil Beast. Natives of North America had
hundreds of different names for this creature, including Mat Log, Devil Beast,
and Sasquatch. But it wasn't until the mid 1950's that the term "Bigfoot" was
used to describe this mysterious being. First identifying and then agreeing on a
name was the first step in trying to understand this misunderstood species.

In the Rocky Mountains, there have been thousands of documented Bigfoot
sightings. One of the most remarkable stories occurred when a prospector by the
name of Albert Ostman went hunting for bear but found a much-bigger surprise.
The old-timer told friends: "My troubles all began in November of 1923, on the
slopes of Bishop Mountain. One morning I awoke to find my campsite dishev-
eled. A nocturnal visitor had rummaged through my belongings and had stolen
sacks of flour and sugar. But once I discovered my last bag of coffee had vanished,
I knew chipmunks weren't to blame. That night I crawled into my sleeping bag,
prepared for battle. I wore my long johns and cowboy boots, in case I had to bolt
from cover. By my side, I kept a canteen of whiskey and a trusty shotgun. I
planned to lie in wait and then ambush the marauding thief. But the sandman got
the best of me. Around midnight, something scooped up my sleeping bag like a
sack of potatoes and carried me downhill! Dazed and confused, I could hear my

A rare photograph of prospector Albert Ostman.
Author's Collection.

captor's labored breathing. But I pretended to be asleep. After a long and uncomfortable journey, I tumbled from my bedroll and found myself surrounded by four huge, apelike creatures! I had to pinch myself to prove I wasn't dreaming. The tallest was a male who stood between nine and ten feet tall. He had a proud, muscular physique. His broad shoulders supported a barrel chest and humped back. Rippling biceps tapered to his elbows while his massive arms hung to his knees. Covered in fur, he stank to high heaven. This muscular fellow seemed to be the leader. At his side was a wide-eyed female, who likely wondered why her hubby had dragged home a crumpled human. The mother monster was about seven feet tall. She had broader hips and walked with a goose-like strut. I could see that she was built more for beauty than for power. She grunted 'Oank-Oank,' which must have been a formal greeting, and I soon realized that the brazen beasts were more interested in studying me than in having Albert Ostman over toast for breakfast! Through grunts and hand signals, I came to understand that I could have my freedom just as long as I didn't leave camp. But all the while, I watched for any chance to escape. My golden opportunity came one week later. After sharing a simple meal of sweet grass and wild berries with my hairy hosts, I grabbed a pinch of chewing tobacco for dessert. With great enthusiasm, I smacked my lips and this intrigued the papa monster, who then grabbed the tempting tin of cherry chew and lapped at the container with an eager tongue. But within moments the tangy treat sickened his stomach, and the great creature let out a horrifying cry of agony. His fierce eyes bulged and rolled to the back of his bulbous head like a guttered bowling ball. During the confusion that followed, I broke free of camp and ran into the woods, without ever looking back over my shoulder! Once I returned to civilization, I swore I'd never tell a single soul about my surreal deliverance from impending doom, as I didn't want to be a laughing stock. But I've since had a change of heart and have decided to come forward with my story, and I'd swear on a stack of holy Bibles that my word is nothing but truth!"

Albert never struck it rich during his lifetime, but he was happy to have become famous for blowing the whistle on Bigfoot. His sensational story was syndicated in newspapers around the world. Come to find out, Ostman wasn't the only human being to have been captured by the big-footed bogey. An old Indian woman also came forward, saying, "When I was a young child, I was kidnapped by a clan of hairy, humanlike creatures and held hostage in a rock-shelter for an entire year before I managed to escape." Her harrowing experience was published on April Fool's Day of 1929, in an article for *Maclean's Magazine* called "Introducing B. C.'s Hairy Giants." But no one was laughing when the account was written as a true story, and shock waves rippled around the world!

Although kidnappings by Bigfoot haven't been reported in recent years, belief in this mysterious creature is on the rise. Hopefully, one day, modern-day scientists will have a name and an answer for this ever-illusive creature. Do you believe?

CROWN JEWELS OF THE ROCKIES

Whenever the art of medicine is loved,
there also is love of humanity.

—Hippocrates

Everyone knows the Rockies are a treasure trove of natural minerals and precious metals. But few folks may realize that ancient medicine can also be mined from ancient mountains. Especially powerful in veterinary medicine is a benign-looking rock known as a Mad Stone. These rare gems saved hundreds of lives before there was a vaccine against rabbis. Denver, Colorado, is home to three such treasured Mad Stones, known as the Crown Jewels of the Rockies.

One of these special rocks saved the life of a precocious boy who one day grew up to become governor. His story began on July 2, 1899, when *Poor Richard's Almanac* noted that the Dog Star was in its ascendancy. This zenith always preceded the dog days of summer. Thank heaven the circus was in town to help folks forget about the stellar heat wave. Although the admittance line snaked around three city blocks, tickets were selling like hotcakes. But little Robert "Bobby" Dean of 420 Easy Street didn't have a wooden nickel to his name. So, the freeloader crawled under the red-and-white-striped tent when nobody was looking and got in for nothing.

Without cash for peanuts, the precocious youth tossed the elephant a quid of chewing tobacco and chuckled at the monster's hideous reaction. The Goliath bellowed, tugged at his chain, and tried to get at Bobby. But the escape artist slipped into the crowd and disappeared like Houdini. At the Bearded Fat Lady exhibit, the curious boy gawked until he couldn't see straight. By that time, he'd forgotten about the naughty prank he'd pulled on the ivory-horned monster. But elephants never forget. Moments later, Bobby felt something cold and clammy, clamp round his scrawny neck. The next thing you know, the elephant's intent trunk threw him into a nearby haystack! In front of the lion's cage, the curious kid slipped an eager hand through the bars to pet a panther. When the lion tamer noticed the brazen boy stealing his thunder, the shirtless man in red tights booted him from the big top.

On his way home, Bobby stopped to bully a mad dog and was bit upon the nose. "Hydrophobia" trumped the police chief in a blue cap. "I've seen these symptoms many times before . . . red ligature marks around the neck and brown-stained teeth . . . not to mention glassy eyes and frothing at the mouth . . . You'll be dead before sunrise— unless . . . unless . . . we can get you treatment with a Mad Stone. It's your only hope!"

Bobby was unaware of the emergency as he growled and barked at anyone who came near him. Alarmed, the police chief threw the boy a bone and shouted, "This is a race against death! Call the doctor at once, and tell him it's an emergency!"

Hours later, the specialist arrived with doctoring bag in hand. Upon a table he unfolded a red-satin cloth, holding a heart-shaped stone. Dr. Leeson placed the porous, black rock in a bucket of warm, sudsy water, saying, "I think the boy might live . . . But, it's a *tuff* call. Most cases of hydrophobia take up to six weeks to advance to this dangerous stage. Why, I once heard a story about a hydrophobia victim in El Paso, whose symptoms didn't manifest until eight years after being bitten by a mad polecat! Still, this boy is lucky to have early intervention. I'm using a trusted Mad Stone recovered from an ancient Indian burial mound. For many years it belonged to an Indian shaman who made his home in the Superstition Mountains, and I inherited the stone from him. I benefit a great deal from its magical powers. Anyways, I'm glad to be of service," the physician said with a wink.

After rolling up starched shirtsleeves, the good doctor removed the Mad Stone from the sudsy bucket. He then boiled the black rock in a pot of goat's milk until it blanched as white as the steaming liquid. Meanwhile, he scraped Bobby's nose with a surgical scalpel, enticing the scab to bleed. Once the soggy rock was placed upon Bobby's bleeding nose, the Mad Stone sucked like a hungry babe on a mother's tit. Dr. Leeson chuckled, saying, "By gum, I've never seen that rock drink with more enthusiasm or voracity. I imagine that the deadly poison from hydrophobia was already coursing through the kid's veins . . . It's a darn good thing we got him treatment, or he would have surely been a goner! Why, I don't know where I'd be without this handy tool in my shed. Mad Stones can be used for curing anything from stubborn boils to toenail fungus. These sacred totems come in handy when extracting deadly venom from poisonous bites. In fact, an infamous snake charmer by the name of Reverend Bill Scroggins often relied on the magical powers of his precious Mad Stone. The preacher used the magic rock for paranormal defense! In fact, he once frightened off a ghost just by shaking his Mad Stone in the phantom's face! Yes sir, a Mad Stone can be a man's best friend," he boasted with a warm smile.

After adhering to Bobby's swollen nose for seven hours, the engorged rock turned black and rolled to the floor. Puffy pores in the stone oozed a greenish goo. So again, Dr. Leeson repeated the procedure.

The next night, Bobby was back at the circus. Only this time, as star attraction. A fat man in a top hat announced: MEET BOBBY DEAN THE WONDER BOY . . . BITTEN BY A DEVIL DOG AND CURED BY A POISON-SUCKING MAD STONE! The crowd roared with anticipation until a rogue elephant charged center ring, wrapped his revengeful trunk around the boy's neck, and tossed him into a nearby haystack. (Circus elephants always got cranky during dog days of summer.)

Fifteen years later, dog days of summer still made circus elephants cranky, and naughty boys were still picking fights with mad dogs. But citizens of Denver were at least relieved to be given an authentic Mad Stone. On January 13, 1914, headlines for the *Denver Post* screamed:

RABID DOG SCARE

REVEALS MAD STONE OWNED IN DENVER

Mrs. Coffman Sends Talisman to Mayor

For Benefit of Victims.

Then, on September 12, 1920, the newspaper revealed yet another generous act of philanthropy. The widow of J. A. Israel, US marshal for Colorado under President Cleveland, donated her marvelous Mad Stone. Her husband's will stated that the rock was to be used by all who might be bitten, and the Israel Stone soon became more famous than the Hope Diamond!

Today, these magic rocks are in a collection known as the Crown Jewels of the Rockies, and they're kept at Governor Hickenlooper's Denver office. And just as in times of old, they are still available to the public as free medical care. However, demand is high, and so an appointment must be made seven years in advance. But just like seeing the greatest show on earth, a sucking session with a magic rock from the Rockies is well worth the wait!

YELLOWSTONE FEVER

Truth can be stranger than fiction.
—Adapted from Mark Twain quote

Have you ever suffered from Yellowstone Fever? If you had, then you'd never forget the harrowing experience. Old Silver Tip had the dubious distinction of being the first victim to identify Yellowstone Fever. One afternoon he was spouting off to a group of children on a school field trip when he said,"Greetings happy campers, and welcome to the world's first national park. My name is Old Silver Tip and I've been giving tours in Yellowstone since I was still wet behind the ears. The Cheyenne people told that the Great Spirit sculpted this valley out of a buffalo hide. They also believed that evil spirits dwelled within the park, and they shunned the area as being taboo. One of the strangest mysteries here at Yellowstone Lake is the sound of an ethereal harp. This haunting music has been blamed for dozens of mysterious deaths. One of the first inexplicable boating accidents occurred on July 4, 1894, when a party of three men took a rowboat filled with beer out on Yellowstone Lake to celebrate Uncle Sam's birthday. Witnesses claimed that as the revelers pushed their boat away from the shoreline, they were playing the harmonica, beating drums, and singing songs. The next day, their splintered boat was found crashed upon the rocks of Stevenson Island, but the three men never resurfaced. Authorities pondered the situation and wondered if shameless sea sirens were to blame. According to Greek legend, sea sirens played haunting harp music that caused boats to crash upon the rocks. Shipwrecked victims would be dragged into underwater lairs where naughty nymphs used seamen to satisfy their unquenchable, carnal lust. Suspicions about sea sirens came to a head in 1910, when a naked skeleton was discovered on Stevenson Island. Apparently, the lusty ladies jumped the victim's bones and then stole away in his rowboat!"

Old Silver Tip glanced around at his wide-eyed audience, sipped rum from a tin cup, burped, and boasted, "You may have noticed that I'm wearing a black

Old Silver Tip was afflicted with Yellowstone Fever.
Author's collection.

eye patch. No, I'm not a pirate. I lost my left eye while boating on Yellowstone Lake. I remember hearing harp music. But I don't recall being pulled underwater by a brazen blonde. After being used and abused, my empty eye socket was fitted with a porcelain imposter, and I was prouder of that glass eye than a peacock is of fancy feathers. One day I was fishing here at Yellowstone Lake, and as I sat in the boat, I popped out my glass eyeball and admired it for a spell. As I was rolling it around in the palm of my hand, it slipped and into the water it went. As the ball sank, it turned to stare at me and then to an approaching shadow . . . It was Old Lucifer himself, the meanest cutthroat trout ever known to mankind. Quick as scat, I dropped a line and landed a hook right before the tremendous trout. As luck would have it, Old Lucifer latched onto the bait. But upon landing my happy prize, I fell overboard! Dangling from my hook was nothing but a glaring eyeball! Now, the fish eye was every bit as big as my natural eye, and the more I looked upon it, the more I thought about how similar it was to my own. So, I stuck that black-rimmed golden iris into the same socket where my custom-made imposter once belonged and it fit, just as snug as a bug in a rug. The only difference was that Lucifer's eye looked wicked. Even so, I reasoned that it might be fun sporting an evil eye. I never complained and said it was still a fair trade, although the limply lamp made everything look dark and cloudy. Then one fine day, I went swimming, and, remarkably, I could see perfectly underwater! I suppose that was reasonable since God didn't create trout eyes to be wandering all over the landscape. Anyway, I enjoyed swimming around, observing aquatic life. But then I came face to face with Old Lucifer himself, and that devilish fish was proudly sporting my glass eyeball! Knowing he couldn't see through the lens, I took full advantage of the situation by grabbing him by the gills! During the terrible tussle, we were both hit on our noggins and darkness struck us at once, like a candle being snuffed from a flame. After the blinding battle, I fished by ear. Thankfully, Old Lucifer was a soprano trout. Soprano trout can sing with the best of them, but they are difficult to hook. Perhaps that's why Lucifer has lived to be older than sin. One time, I reeled in the dirty devil. But the testy trout spit in my good eye and made a quick escape! Until that day, I'd never heard a fish cuss!"

Old Silver Tip swatted a mosquito that was bigger than the average jackalope and then continued spinning his yarn by saying, "Yes sir, Yellowstone is a mysterious place. But come to find out, there's a darn good reason for all of this madness. This park stands on a 'super volcano,' known as the 'Yellowstone Caldera.' Big-brained scientists agree that seismic activity produces a change in electromagnetic waves, and this peculiar pulse causes problems. Unpredictable animal behavior is a huge concern. Why, just last week, an experienced hunter was accidently shot to death by his trigger-happy bloodhound. This crazed thinking in animals and humans has since become known as Yellowstone Fever. The first symptom of this strange malady is a lack of a common sense. One good example occurred in the summer of 1902. A dance was being held at the Yellowstone Lake Hotel, when an amorous young couple stepped outside for a romantic stroll in the woods. Suddenly from out of nowhere came a lost baby bear, whining in fear and longing for maternal love. The young man felt sorry for the little tyke, and so he cuddled the cub in his coat, dried its tears, and sang a comforting lullaby. Next thing you know, the absentee momma bear came along and tore the babysitter to shreds. Luckily, the young woman managed to escape before being gobbled for dessert! Obviously, her dim-witted companion was a victim of Yellowstone Fever; otherwise he wouldn't have tried making friends with a hungry grizzly. Although there still isn't a known cure, Yellowstone Fever can be easily avoided by using just a little self-restraint and common sense, especially when it comes to snuggling with baby bears . . .

"Well, happy campers, my time is up. But remember this wise advice. Don't pet wild animals or eat yellow snow! And . . . good luck hooking that one-eyed soprano!"

GHOST WALTZ OF FORT UNION

Dance me to the end of Love.

—Leonard Cohen

Along the Santa Fe Trail were once several military posts built by Uncle Sam. Fort Union was an appropriate name for a fortress that united friends and foes for miles around. Built on the border at a time of civil unrest among the Mexicans, Americans, and native Indians, the outpost brought safety and security to many. Fort Union was an open post, a rarity in that it was designed without stockades or outcroppings of any kind. And it appeared to be a friendly place, which looked more like an inviting frontier village than a strict military installation. History books will tell you that this utopia was unknowingly built on private property designated by the Morrow Land Grant, and that's why it was soon deserted. But now you'll learn the real reason why the old military outpost was quickly abandoned.

This mystery all began shortly after the fort was erected. When on a stormy night came the first babe to be born. The captain's Apache wife died while giving birth to this unfortunate child, and thus an apparent curse fell over the fortress. Three dairy cows mysteriously died the night Lucinda came into the world. Those in tune with the higher laws of nature determined that this was a terrible omen and that the child was born inherently evil. As she grew, Lucinda didn't talk much, and she always kept to herself. Whispers around sewing circles told that the captain's kid was twitched in the head, and many feared she was bewitched. At least everyone could agree that the mixed-race girl was a misfit. As an outcast, she seemed to live in a world of her own making, with her head in the clouds. But nobody dared say much since she was the captain's only child.

Over the years, Lucinda's haunting beauty blossomed. Illustrious black hair cascaded down her back and framed her large, dark eyes. Proudly, she flaunted her willowy figure, and her seductive innocence drew men to Fort Union like bees to honey. But none of the bachelors ever dared ask to court the witchy woman, because they feared her overly protective father and her innate mystery.

One day, Lucinda learned of a masquerade party to be held at the fort. So, she went to work sewing a slinky red flamenco dress with matching head veil. Mouths dropped when she made her grand entrance into the mess hall, and every soldier at Fort Union endeavored to dance with the mysterious belle of the ball.

One glass of sangria led to another, and Lucinda soon fell head over heels for a handsome lieutenant. Tall, dark, and handsome is what all the ladies called Lieutenant Dan. Being that he was also half Apache, he seemed the perfect match for dark and lovely Lucinda. The couple looked like a match made in heaven, as they swayed together while the mariachi band played. Until the stroke of midnight, when double doors to the mess hall swung open and a soldier riding a fine, black stallion charged onto the dance floor with an urgent message! The Apaches had attacked a nearby pioneer settlement. Naturally, Lieutenant Dan was put in charge of the rescue mission. But before leaving, he made a sacred promise that he'd soon return to marry his soulmate, and that he'd always love Lucinda through a calendar of time.

Night and day, Lucinda sat at her bedroom window and faithfully awaited for her fiancé's return. Alas, the detachment finally did return to the fortress. But they did so without the love-struck lieutenant.

"He got cold feet and ran for the hills," teased one of his soldiers. "That armchair Romeo eloped with a drunken dance hall girl," sassed another.

Finally, with a heavy heart, Lucinda reluctantly agreed to marry the lieutenant's much-older, half-dead, half brother.

The mess hall was decorated with delicate paper hearts cut from burlap and brown mailing paper. Empty whiskey bottles held colorful wildflowers. As lovely Lucinda swayed gently in an old man's arms, she was embarrassed for her situation. Desperately she tried to smile as guests threw coins on the sweeping dance floor. It was a joyous affair, but not for Lucinda, who grew colder with each passing kiss. Suddenly, a bitter howling swept across the chamber, and every candle in the hall was hushed into darkness. Stewards hastily relit tapers as the band nervously played on. And then, at the sudden stroke of midnight, double doors to the mess hall flung wide open, and a black stallion stormed onto the dance floor! Upon the steed sat a wounded soldier in bloodied uniform. Guitars, tambourines, and horns came to a screeching halt. Every eye turned to see the ghoulish fiend, who was soon recognized as the missing lieutenant! He'd been scalped, and the angry blade of a tomahawk still dangled precariously from his forehead! With throbbing temples, worms slithered from the dead man's vacant eye sockets! And as wide-eyed guests sat spellbound in silence, the wicked fiend threw back his head with unhinged laughter. With a mechanical goose step, the ghoul began a slow march toward the stunned couple. You'd think anyone with half a brain would have bolted for the doors. But the crowd was under the influence of a strange, hypnotic spell. Guests sat paralyzed with fear as they watched in horrific apprehension. Then, without saying a word, the dead man grabbed his much older, half-dead, half-brother by his scrawny neck and promptly squeezed the living tarnation out of him. With a resounding thud, the elderly groom fell dead on the dance floor, as his revengeful brother smiled with toothless gums. With a wicked laugh, the lieutenant's corpse then grabbed his unhappy prize with a willful kiss! And with a snap of bony fingers, a hypnotized band picked up their instruments and began playing the Wedding Waltz! Round and round the couple swirled and twirled as drop-jawed guests gazed in silent wonder. Once the song ended, a dizzied bride was released from a devilish clutch and away she tumbled. Lucinda then sank to the floor like a deflated balloon, heaving her last breath just as the phantom lieutenant vanished into thin air!

Had it all been some sort of wild, collective dream? Fort Union's physician, who wasn't at the horror show, claimed the bride and groom had both died from sudden heart failure brought on by nervous tension, and he left it at that. But wedding guests knew better. Even so, nobody ever questioned the good doctor or mentioned the unthinkable tragedy until a few days later, when a party of friendly natives approached with incredible news. They'd found the missing soldier . . . rotting on a nearby hillside. Lieutenant Dan had been struck between the eyes by an Apache tomahawk!

News about the ghost waltz spread far and wide, and it wasn't long before Fort Union became known as a terribly wicked place. As night after night, soldiers were awakened by haunting music . . . the Wedding Waltz. And it got to the point where nobody wanted to live within the haunted keep. Obviously, the union was over, and it wasn't long before the fortress was shuttered and forever abandoned by all except for its ghosts.

Today, Fort Union is a historic landmark visited both by the living and the dead, which is a gentle way of saying that, yes, the Ole Homestead is still spook infested. Legend tells that a haunting Wedding Waltz can still be heard drifting

through abandoned adobe walls, long after the band's stopped playing. And on nights of the full moon, two ghosts can still be seen waltzing through the long-abandoned courtyard, and they're both grooms! Nobody seems to know why Lucinda's miserable spirit hasn't joined the two brothers' phantom dance, but then again she was always considered a little strange. And as this paranormal party continues through a calendar of time, it seems that the union at Fort Union really isn't over after all!

The birth of baby Lucinda brought death, and a supernatural curse fell over Fort Union. *Author's collection.*

WEIRD CURSE OF
MANITOU SPRINGS

God moves in a mysterious way, His wonders to perform.
—William Cowper

Manitou Springs is weird. But at least there's good reason why. The strangeness began with a heated argument long ago. Two Native Americans from warring tribes stood on opposite sides of a holy mineral spring. One boasted that he deserved the first sip because his people were superior. Naturally, the other warrior disagreed. One insult led to another, and blood was spilled over the bubbling waters of Fountain Creek. Murderous cries echoed throughout the sacred valley as streaks of lightning and booming thunder rattled Arcadian skies. From his heavenly throne in the happy hunting grounds, the Great Spirit bellowed, "HOLY WATERS ARE TO BE SHARED BY ONE AND ALL. AS PUNISHMENT FOR YOUR GREED, THIS SACRED VALLEY WILL BE CURSED, UNTIL FURTHER NOTICE!"

In the 1860s, wagon trains rolled into the sacred valley as the white man chased Cheyenne, Shoshone, Ute, Kiowa, and Apache Indians away from their ancestral hunting grounds. Happy homesteads sprouted along the gurgling waters of Fountain Creek. But paradise was soon lost when flocks of hungry locusts and herds of ravenous earthworms feasted on budding crops. The pioneers worried after learning of the ancient Indian curse. So, they christened the valley "Manitou," which was an Indian word meaning the "Great Spirit." This respectful gesture placated the gods until greedy entrepreneurs began making big bucks off the sacred valley.

The Manitou Bottling Company was one of the first businesses to exploit the holy waters. Crates of bottled Manitou Water and Ginger Champagne shipped around the world for a nifty profit. But when the unsinkable *Titanic* sank along with a case of Manitou mineral water, everyone, including the White Star Line, blamed the Manitou Bottling Company. Of course it wasn't long before the thriving company soon went bankrupt. Then the Manitou Bath House commercialized the sacred springs by renting warm water to dirty tourists. But not long after hanging their shingle, the owner was found murdered, and the bath house burned to ashes. Also lost to mysterious fires were several grand hotels. Coincidently, all these fine establishments exploited Manitou spring water. Newspapers from coast to coast noted the irony, and once again, smoldering embers stirred about the ancient Indian curse.

After pestilence and fire came the so-called White Plague. The only known remedy was living in a dry climate and drinking plenty of spring water. Desperate tuberculosis patients flocked to Manitou hoping for a cure. Victims looked more dead than alive, and their gruesome appearance was hard to forget. Fingernails turned brown, while the whites of eyes yellowed. Hair loss and skin rash was common. Scratching caused oozing sores, and thirsty leaches were used to suck out deadly infection. Labored lungs collected mucus and blood, which leaked from trembling lips and dribbled down chins. Because skeletal victims looked like the walking dead, they were referred to as "vampires." A tin cup was tied over each watering hole, and every evening, vampires would creep from one spring to the next, under the discreet cloak of darkness.

But sharing a common drinking cup spread the plague like wildfire. Fear became epidemic in itself. Tuberculosis patients wore cow bells around their necks, warning of their deadly condition. Sanitariums overflowed, and so a few generous millionaires converted their palatial mansions into charitable hospitals. Quarantine rooms and private porches were built onto residential houses. Once all beds were filled, canvas tents and primitive tree-limb shelters crowded hillsides. Although illegal shanties caused a serious fire hazard, poor sanitation became a far-greater threat. Proper hygiene was encouraged by nurses who visited the living dead at hillside shacks. Vampires were encouraged to gain weight by drinking at least three liters of whole milk and swallowing dozens of raw eggs daily. Vomit and blood puddled along sidewalks and public gardens. Also spoiling the fresh, alpine air were stinking corpses, piled high. At one time, the dead far outnumbered the living, and busied undertakers couldn't keep up with the grueling demand for proper burials.

One corpse without a grave was a vampire by the name of Miss Emma Crawford, a world-famed pianist. Young, talented, and beautiful, the Angel of Death showed the wealthy socialite no mercy. Emma's loving fiancé refused to keep her corpse on ice until she could be properly buried in the town cemetery. So, he hiked to the top of Red Mountain during midwinter and illegally dug a dismal hole for his belated bride. It took twelve pallbearers working in two shifts to deliver the tiny, gray casket to the summit. During the arduous journey, pulley ropes snapped and launched Emma into snowbanks and icy gullies. Upon reaching the summit, she was buried under a pile of rocks and a wind-swept piñon tree. But darling

Emma never rested in peace. Shortly after her strange funeral, Red Mountain became haunted. Weird piano music drifted from the cliffs of Red Mountain, and Emma's luminous ghost could be seen dancing upon the moonlit summit.

News about the resurrected vampire-ghost made national headlines. Conniving capitalists took advantage of Emma's new fame by erecting the Red Mountain Incline. Although the cog railroad was built in haste and wasn't structurally sound, tourists eagerly paid a steep fee and risked their lives just for the chance of communicating with the dead. Worried adventurists packed picnic baskets stuffed with holy water, wooden stakes, and garlic sandwiches. Devout spiritualists brought Manitou Spirit Boards, Manitou Fortune-Telling Cards, and Manitou Crystal Balls. Hordes of tourists paid big bucks to have their photographs taken with Manitou's famous vampire-ghost. Novelties such as Emma Crawford back scratchers and snow globes sold like buckets of tea leaves.

Celebrated psychics and paranormal enthusiasts came from around the country to investigate the prolific hauntings of Manitou Springs. After noticing confused crows circling above town, these experts recognized pockets of peculiar magnetic anomalies. Their trusted compass began spinning in circles, never landing on true north. That's when famed Serbian scientist Nikola Tesla noted that most of the town's buildings were constructed from a rare rock known as Manitou greenstone. And how Manitou greenstone was found only in Manitou Springs and contained weird magnetic properties. Apparently, this powerful draw caused migratory birds to lose their innate sense of direction and attracted ghosts to the Victorian village.

Then came the master of all disasters. Deadly floods washed through the haunted town shortly after the fancy Manitou Spa arose upon the banks of Fountain Creek. The massive structure commercialized Manitou's largest and most sacred spring. Concerned city leaders hoped to appease ancient gods of the Ute, Arapahoe Kiowa, Apache, and Cheyenne by erecting a clock tower in name of the Great Spirit Manitou. Above the number 12 stood a bronze statue. The naked Greek goddess poured the breath of Manitou from a tipped urn, and these bubbly waters flowed into a pool of tossed pennies. But this dismal peace offering only aggravated the Great Spirit Manitou, who sent torrential waters that continually tormented the town.

In 1999, the flooded spa building was saved from the wrecking ball and restored back to its former glory. But before the ribbon cutting, developers welcomed spiritual leaders from the American Indian nation; they held a healing rite over the Manitou Spa and its namesake village. After the sacred ceremony, five squawking crows flew away from the tiled roof and into a closed window, sending glass shards in every direction but north. Tribal leaders bowed their heads in reverence and noted that the ancient curse had been lifted. But only for a short while. Thirteen years later, angry floods again ravaged the town, and city leaders feared that the weird Indian hoodoo was to blame.

After many years of trial and tribulation, the Manitou Springs Chamber of Commerce resolved to embrace their problem rather than trying to dismiss the ancient spell. Their new public-relations campaign promised to "Keep Manitou Weird," and this became the village's motto. The Great Spirit smiled down from his heavenly throne in the happy hunting grounds.

Today, Manitou Springs is still really weird, likely because the village is home to writers, dancers, actors, singers, painters, and musicians . . . in a nutshell, artists. Diversity is celebrated and creative license is freely given. Sips from the sacred springs are also free of charge. But you'll want to bring your own cup, because nobody wants to swap cooties with a bunch of weirdos!

FEAR OF SHEEP MOUNTAIN

There is more in the universe that we don't understand
than what we do.

—Unknown

Do you believe extraterrestrial beings have visited our planet? During the late 1800s, hundreds of wide-eyed witnesses were dizzied by roving aircraft seen hovering over the Rockies. And some of these recollections came from sober people. The accounts happened decades before the Wright brothers took flight over Kitty Hawk. Could it be that we earthlings are not alone? According to the popular television program *Ancient Aliens*, extraterrestrial beings might be attracted to rich mineral deposits found in the Rocky Mountains. Perhaps that's why many of these early sightings were seen over mining camps. One of the first official reports was featured in the *Rocky Mountain News*. And how it became published happened something like this . . .

After taking off his cowboy hat, Sam Stump sat before the chief editor of the *Rocky Mountain News*. The rancher was nervous and it clearly showed, as he was squirming in his chair like he had ants in his pants.

A fat man in a dark suit took one look at the greenhorn and chuckled, saying, "You look like you have a story to tell! I've heard many in my day. Speak up. I'm all ears."

After biting his lip, the young man sheepishly mumbled, "Thank you, kindly. I've come from a great distance. Over hill and dale and through rain, sleet, and hail. And yes, I have big news. Strange as it may be. It all began several years ago . . . We've been experiencing supernatural hoodoo in our neck of the woods. When I say we, I mean ranchers, farmers, and what not. I'm here as a representative from our peaceful community. At least it was serene until our citizens began disappearing. Vaporized without a trace! And it wasn't just people. We also noticed cattle had gone missing. Later we'd find them in a bad way. Lying on their backs with all fours sticking up in midair—stiff as a board. As you

The fear of Sheep Mountain was first discovered
by a rancher known as Mr. Stump, seen here in a rare photograph.
Author's Collection.

likely know, predators and scavengers tear flesh from bones with great fearsomeness. But the heart, lungs, brains, liver, and sexual organs had been delicately extracted with a straight blade! All blood had been drained—not a drop spilled! Sometimes we noted a slimy substance. This pea-green jelly burned to the touch and was itchy upon our skin. Large, perfect circles burned into the prairie grass surrounded the carcasses.

"After ruling out coyotes and wolves, we assumed pranksters were to blame. But these attacks also happened to our neighbor's livestock, and besides, why would anybody go to such great extremes for a joke? Everyone knows you could get shot for fiddling with a rancher's livestock. Anyway, we noticed a connection between the slaughtered cattle and mysterious lights seen hovering in night skies.

"A few weeks ago, hundreds of drop-jawed witnesses spotted roving aircraft over Cripple Creek, during broad daylight! Flashing lights flew from east to west and then north to south. Different colors, shapes, and sizes . . . It was really something. And we've been seeing them over Sheep Mountain!

"A few days ago, I got brave and decided to investigate. Near the top of a ridge I discovered a dead mule. At first I surmised it got stuck in the bramble and starved to death. From around the neck it was tied to a tree, and it'd been cut to pieces! Circling buzzards told me the beast hadn't been dead long. A fine saddle was still strapped to its back! Hand tooled with silver filigree adornments, probably from Mexico. Nobody in their right mind would leave a costly saddle behind. Or tie a beast of burden to a tree and let it starve. And the native Utes would never let good meat spoil! No sir. I reckoned something sinister was at play. So, I took the saddle off the beast and hid it under a bush, planning to fetch it later. And then I continued my journey. But not for long. Just around the bend I discovered another dead animal. This time the mule was tethered to a rock. Again, it was saddled and violated. Must have happened fast, too, because the ground was still moist. But not with blood. Wet with jelly that stung my fingers like jalapeño juice!

"Goose bumps rippled down my hide. I cared not to explore further without the expertise of a professional. So I spurred my hoss and turned home. Bud Burrows was the keenest tracker this side of the Platte. So we packed a couple of mules with provisions and made our way back up Sheep Mountain, which is really more of a molehill. Near a stretch of red crags was another dead mule. It'd been tied to a tree stump and was mutilated. Gunny sacks hanging from its fleshless frame held flour, sugar, and coffee. There was another sack of pots and pans. Inside a leather satchel was a man's yellow rain slicker, the kind a ship captain might wear. And a woman's knitted poncho in the dark shade of blue. But nothing else was noted. Except the eerie feeling that washed over us like a lead balloon. It felt like we were being watched or studied from afar. And we both noticed the uncanny feeling. Our knees were knocking and teeth chattering. But neither of us wanted to admit we were frightened. Throwing caution to the winds, we soldiered on. Moments later, we were sitting on the summit and all alone. Our mules were gone. Somehow they'd been taken from beneath us while we were still riding them! Neither of us had recollection of what had happened. Our pocket watches were broken. Frozen at 11:11, which was the same time we'd moseyed past the crags. Nothing made sense. Especially because we were surrounded by a large, circular patch of burnt grass and we itched like we'd been bitten by an army of fleas!"

After hearing Sam Stump's frightful tale, the newspaper sent a research team to investigate. Reporters agreed that something strange was at play. But the mystery has never been solved.

And so it was that Sheep Mountain became feared both by man and beast! Even today, locals are still sheepish about Sheep Mountain . . . and can you blame them?

TRUTH OR CONSEQUENCES AND THE SPANISH FLY

The best-laid plans of mice and men go oft awry.
—Robert Burns

Early Spanish explorers first recognized the Hassayampa as a liar. The sandy river seemingly flows upside-down and is much deeper than it appears. In the late 1800s, the Hassayampa flooded and eighteen victims died. Poor engineering of a river dam was to blame. But shifty lawyers argued it was just a silly accident, and those at fault walked away scot-free. Legend tells us that ever since this grave injustice, all who drink from the Hassayampa River will become habitual liars!

Ernest Malarkey despised liars, since his parents died in the senseless tragedy. With a dark heart, Ernest left everything behind, and Turtleback Mountain became his new home. The oldster found refuge in a spring-fed cave, where chipmunks and squirrels licked his wounds. Like Henry David Thoreau nesting upon Walden Pond, the hermit became one with nature. He collected clover honey, wild berries, and animal skins, which were traded for household essentials such as flour, sugar, and coffee. Once supplies dwindled, Ernest would ride his faithful donkey into the nearest village, known as Truth or Consequences. At the general store he did his shopping and hobnobbed with fellow mountain men. By October, old man Malarkey would be snowbound.

The winter of 1879 was no exception. Sometimes the oldster would get mighty lonely for company. His prayers were answered when, on Christmas morning, the jingling of happy bells clanged upon his door. Could it be jolly Old Saint Nick? No, silly reader. Why would Santa be making deliveries on Christmas morning? The red-nosed intruder brazenly buzzed inside, and no, he wasn't named Rudolph. The drunkard introduced himself as Don Juan and sang "Feliz Navidad" while shaking a tiny tambourine. Malarkey had never seen such a miniscule musical instrument. He found it peculiar that Don Juan was playing his favorite Christmas carol, and stranger still that the musical housefly was alive in midwinter.

"Excuse me, amigo," demurred the debonair insect. "But I was lured to your lofty abode by the enticing scent of saffron paella . . . I'm also a galloping gourmet . . . I've come from Spain. Do you speak Spanish? I'm bilingual, especially when plied with liquor. I can talk fly as well as the King's English."

Old man Malarkey was speechless. After all, it's not every day that you meet a smooth-talking fly. Especially one as handsome and well-dressed as Don Juan. The Spanish fly had a chilled bottle of sangria tucked under one wing, and a box of fine chocolates under the other. So, in ode to the joy of Christmas, Malarkey invited the passing stranger to stay for supper.

Being that it was a special occasion and all, proper candles were set upon the stone table. Although as different as night and day, the old, Irish hermit and the young, Spanish fly had much in common. For example, both enjoyed hot soup and cold showers. But the happy chatter soon turned dark when the Spaniard got hammered and played a braggart's game. After boasting of many wives and fathering 500 children, the red-faced oldster accused the pompous peacock of sipping from the Hassayampa River! But Don Juan proved to be as honest as the rain in Spain. After hearing the insect's song and dance about how he'd become a political refugee after fighting a bloody revolution against a corrupt government, the old Irishman took sympathy on the Spaniard by offering sanctuary. But Malarkey insisted that it would only be until the snow melted and that Donnie had to agree to house rules:

1. We shall not cuss.
2. Fights shall be settled with words and not fists.
3. We shall not "kid" each other excessively.
4. We shall always abide by the law of cleanliness.
5. We shall always be honest.

Malarkey and Don Juan soon became the best of buds. Ernest enjoyed playing his fiddle for the fly, and the little lothario delighted in dancing the flamenco. Don Juan loved drinking games. But unlike common barflies, the Spaniard could hold his liquor. Sad to say, but the Spaniard often drank the Irishman under the table. Being that he was well read, Don Juan could quote from Plato and Socrates, although he confessed to not knowing much of Robert Burns. But that fact didn't worry the old man, because in his feeble mind Donnie was still a fly. The aspiring intellectuals also dreamed of doing sporty things together such as biking, hunting, and fishing. Malarkey joked that a juicy fly would come in handy at the lake! (But as agreed, teasing wasn't done to excess.) Come early spring, love was in the air. The odd couple looked forward to double dating, and the oldster noted that a little Spanish fly would come in handy with nasty ladies. Yet, as Robert Burns once said, the best-laid plans between mice and men go oft awry. And so it was rather uncanny when fate soon intervened between man and insect.

Ole Malarkey became *a wise lawgiver before giving up the ghost.*
Author's collection.

One morning, Ernest Malarkey awoke to find that a new neighbor had moved into his armpit. Without thinking, he broke commandment number one. Bradford T. Bedbug had never heard an old man cuss, and it took him off guard. On bended knee the bedbug begged for Malarkey's ear. And with bloodied fangs he stuttered that he was in a bad way and needed new digs. His wife had kicked him out and he'd been sleeping on a dog's tail.

Ernest listened patiently. But after the bedbug mentioned that he was an attorney by trade, Malarkey saw red! Malarkey hated liars *and* lawyers! Yet, after looking into the bedbug's pleading eyes, Ernest took pity on the vagabond and welcomed him into his home. But the reluctant host was emphatic that Bradford could stay only for one night, knowing that bedbugs always hogged the covers and all.

Don Juan was nowhere to be seen or heard. So the old man just assumed his little buddy was sleeping off another one of his horrible hangovers. Old man Malarkey and Brad the bedbug had a riotous time playing board games. But all the hooting and hollering finally woke the Spanish fly. So, the fly buzzed over to the kitchen table and sat upon the butt of a snuffed cigar. At first the gamers didn't take notice of their sleepy-eyed spectator because they were too busy concentrating on their heated match.

After a little while, Don Juan took interest in the thrilling completion. Without considering the costly risk, the fly slammed five pesos upon the checkerboard, betting his entire alimony payment on his best bud, Ernest Malarkey. As the game progressed, the fly couldn't hold his excitement, and so when old man Malarkey trumped "KING ME," Don Juan buzzed "Olé!"

Brad the bedbug was a sore loser. In a fit of anger, the bedbug jumped the Spanish fly, bit off his head, and sucked his blood and guts before Malarkey could do anything but cry. When the oldster questioned Bradford's deceitful motives, the brazen bedbug snickered that the cold-blooded murder was just a silly accident.

Ernest had heard that miserable excuse before! Without thinking, he grabbed his Winchester and blew the fool's head off and then cried like a baby and babbled, "Woe to me who has committed murder, and this one is most foul. Strange and unnatural. Hasten me to know that I with wings may be swept to my revenge!"

Needless to say, the old man's grief was epic, and he knew that the great bard himself couldn't have written such a sorrowful Shakespearean tragedy. Being raised on prunes and proverbs, Ernest Malarkey had always prided himself as being the greatest lawgiver since Moses. But he'd never considered making drinking, gambling, or murder against house rules.

Come morning, a single grave was dug and Bradford T. Bedbug was buried along with the dismal remains of Don Juan, the Spanish fly. After the mournful funeral, Malarkey hitched his donkey with snowshoes and they tramped down the perilous mountain. In the village of Truth or Consequences, the miserable oldster made his terrible, dark confession. A makeshift jury of six fellow mountain men sat stoically and patiently listened.

Ernest Malarkey stood atop a pickle barrel and lamented about how he'd lost everything, beginning with his peaceful mining cabin on the banks of the Hassayampa River, and how he'd become a sudden orphan. But he was grateful that the terrible tragedy led to the love between him and his pet fly. He claimed that all was bliss, until Bradford the bedbug barged into their happy world and ruined everything.

After pondering evidence and facts of the simple matter, all agreed that the selfish bedbug had it coming. Old Malarkey pled guilty to justifiable homicide, and after he was given a slap on the wrist, court was dismissed. Malarkey took life's lemons and made lemonade by writing a bestselling autobiography. He addressed trouble on the Hassayampa River, and this led to stricter building codes.

Ernest became a hero to many, and so Turtleback Mountain was renamed Malarkey Mountain in his honor. All the media attention inspired soul searchers and teenagers to climb the mountain of Malarkey and beseech the wise old man for sage wisdom. But even with many visitors, Malarkey was still lonely. So, the old man dismissed the Walden Pond lifestyle, claiming that life as a brooding hermit was overrated. Gladly, he moved into Truth or Consequences and adopted a mangy mutt to keep him company. But he instead preferred the friendship of its many fleas.

The following spring, he hit the road, and Ernest Malarkey's Flying Flea Circus brought joy throughout the Rockies! Spectators observed costumed acrobats through tiny telescopes. Every show was a sellout, and it was really something.

Years later, Ernest Malarkey kicked the bucket, and his lucrative estate left millions to a pet insect rescue shelter, the first of its kind. Millions of acrobatic fleas found forever homes. Don Juan also contributed to the progress of mankind, albeit posthumously. Before his untimely death he'd invented an aphrodisiac called "Spanish fly," and it's still used in professional fertility clinics to this very day!

But, READER BEWARE. Because this tall tale, like many others in this anthology, was written by an author who often hikes the mountain of Malarkey and sips from the Hassayampa River!

An old cemetery gate opens to long-forgotten yesterdays.
Photo by Cheryl Oney.

CONCLUSION

Every family has a skeleton in the closet, and ours is a sorrowful rags to riches, to rags again tale, which began about 150 years ago . . . After my great-great-grandfather struck it rich during the Pikes Peak gold rush, he wrote home saying that for generations to come, our family would never want for more. And that he'd soon be home to help celebrate by building a new church! The following night, Grandpa's horse crashed through the barn. "Mug" stood nickering under my grandparent's bedroom window until the sun rose.

My grandmother always wondered if it was the night her beloved husband died. In any case, Grandpa Robinson was never heard from again. His withered bones are likely lying at the bottom of a hole—a victim of claim jumpers who got the gold mine while Gramps got the shaft.

But until the day she died, my great-great-grandmother patiently awaited his happy return. Every night, a single white taper candle was left burning in their bedroom window. She never gave up the ghost, until she finally died of a broken heart. Found in her cold hand was a tear-stained love letter addressed to her long-lost husband, and it was her last wish that this poem be set to music. I'm not a musician, but maybe she'd be happy knowing her sentiments were published posthumously:

I Will Remember Your Love in My Prayers

When the curtains of night are drawn by the stars
And the beautiful moon leaps the skies
And the dewdrops of heaven are kissing the rose
'Tis then when my memory flies
As if on the wings of some beautiful dove
In haste with the message it bears
To bring you a kiss of affection and say
I'll remember your love in my prayers.

Chorus:
To where you will on land or on seas
I'll share all your sorrows and cares
And pray at night when I kneel by my bedside
I'll remember your love in my prayers.

I have loved you too fondly to ever forget
All the love you have spoken for me.
And the kiss of affection still warm on my lips
When you told how true you would be.

I care not if fortune be fickle or friend
As time on my memory wears
I know that I love you wherever you roam
And remember your love in my prayers.

I know there are angels watching over you
And may their bright spirit see you through
And guide you up heaven's bright stairs
To meet with the one who has loved you so true
And remembered your love in her prayers.
—Elizabeth Sofie King Robinson, 1888

This poem became my grandmother's Swan Song, since it took many years to compose and she'd died soon after it was completed. Even after all this time, reading her passionate words still brings a tear to my eye. Once I became a writer of legends and lore, her song served as a persuasive reminder that inspiration was easily found by simply shaking my shady family tree. Perhaps this book will inspire you to look into secrets of your own heritage and ancestry . . .

Thanks for traveling with me through a calender of yesterdays, and may your future be blessed with many more exciting adventures into the past!

Happy Trails,
Stephanie Waters
a.k.a. The Galloping Historian

BIBLIOGRAPHY

Ballinger, Dean W. *Real West Magazine*. Derby, CT: Charlton Publication, July 1963.

Harrison, Michael. *Fire from Heaven*. Rev. ed. London: Skoob Books, 1990.

Vazquez, Clarissa. *Ghost Hunting in Colorado*. CreateSpace, 2011.

Waters, Stephanie. *Colorado Legends & Lore: The Phantom Fiddler, Snow Snakes and Other Tales*. Charleston, SC: History Press, 2014.

Waters, Stephanie. *Forgotten Tales of Colorado*. Charleston, SC: History Press, 2013.

Waters, Stephanie. *Ghosts of Colorado Springs and Pikes Peak*. Charleston, SC: History Press, 2012.

Waters, Stephanie. *Haunted Manitou Springs*. Charleston, SC: History Press, 2011.